{ MIND
HACKING }

MIND
HACKING

How to Change Your Mind for Good in 21 Days

Sir John Hargrave

G

Gallery Books

New York   London   Toronto   Sydney   New Delhi

Gallery Books
An Imprint of Simon & Schuster, Inc.
1230 Avenue of the Americas
New York, NY 10020

The art used on pages 35, 62, 69, and 117 is by dix! Digital Prepress, Inc.; on pages 106 and 107, by Robert Ettlin; on page 199, by Akasha Archer.

First Gallery Books hardcover edition January 2016

For information about special discounts for bulk purchases, please contact Simon & Schuster Special Sales at 1-866-506-1949 or business@simonandschuster.com.

The Simon & Schuster Speakers Bureau can bring authors to your live event. For more information or to book an event, contact the Simon & Schuster Speakers Bureau at 1-866-248-3049 or visit our website at www.simonspeakers.com.

Manufactured in the United States of America

1   3   5   7   9   10   8   6   4   2

Library of Congress Cataloging-in-Publication Data

Hargrave, John.
Mind hacking : how to change your mind for good in 21 days /
Sir John Hargrave.
pages   cm
1. Thought and thinking.   2. Change (Psychology).   I. Title.
BF441.H313   2016
158.1—dc23   2015010851

ISBN 978-1-5011-0565-4
ISBN 978-1-5011-0567-8 (ebook)

{ MIND }
HACKING

```
$numreads = 0;
sub ReadBook {
```

My Story

The day I gave up drinking was the day the Secret Service stormed my living room.

"Stormed" might be too strong a word, since they asked if they could come in first. They were polite about it, two senior agents and a younger guy in his twenties. Maybe I should have said no, but I was still a little buzzed from lunch. It was the Friday before Labor Day, and I had polished off a couple of beers with some coworkers before leaving work early and coming home. I only drank on special occasions, such as weekdays.

At the time, I was running a humor website that was known for doing outrageous stunts to get publicity and promotion. One of my favorite pranks was getting a credit card in a celebrity's name. It was surprisingly easy to do: you just called up your credit card company, told them you wanted to add an "additional cardholder," and gave them a famous person's name. Like, say, Barack Obama.

At the time I got the fake credit card with Barack Obama's name, he had not been officially nominated as a candidate for the 2008 presidential election, but I could see it was likely he'd end up in the Oval Office. So I gleefully wrote up the story of my credit card prank, which brought in loads of traffic to our website. I had been taking bigger and bigger risks with my pranks, trying to outdo myself, and I thought pranking the president was pretty much the pinnacle.

I was right. The day after Obama received the official nomination, the Secret Service were on my doorstep. As they filed in, I led them to the living room, where two of the agents sat on the sofa. I sat on the love seat. The senior agent stood in front of my fireplace, facing me, his arms folded. None of the movie clichés applied: they were not wearing earpieces or sunglasses. Also, they were in *my* living room, which I've never seen in a movie.

"You may not realize that the Secret Service not only protects presidential candidates," explained the agent sitting on my couch, "but we also protect the nation's money supply. So by getting a credit card in Obama's name, *you've put yourself in the crosshairs of what we do*." He was in his mid- to late forties, with a receding hairline and dark, penetrating eyes.

"Identity theft carries a maximum of fifteen years in federal prison," added the stocky agent in front of the fireplace, then looked around. "You've got a beautiful house here, a nice family." He paused. "It would be a shame to throw all that away."

I had been in some insane situations, but my heart was pumping alcohol-fueled adrenaline to my brain. Perhaps that explained the thought running through my mind, which was: *I will not give them the credit card*.

"We'd like the credit card," said the stocky agent, his arms still folded.

My voice was shaking. "I can't do that."

"Yeah? Why not?"

"Technically, the credit card belongs to the credit card company," I replied, citing a little-known legal loophole. "I can't give it to you without their permission."

"We'll call them," said the agent on the couch, dialing the credit card company on his cell phone. Apparently, they had anticipated this.

"One second," I said, and walked to my computer bag, shaky-legged, to get my voice recorder. If I was going to give up my precious credit card, at least I was going to record the conversation so I could write about it on my website.

"What's that?" demanded the stocky one.

"I need to tell you that I will be recording this conversation," I answered, hitting the Record button.

They looked at each other, and with surprising swiftness rose to leave. "This interview is *over*," said the stocky one as they stormed out the door and drove off.

I watched them until they turned the corner, then breathed a huge sigh of relief. Then I calmly walked into the bathroom and puked.

That night was one of the worst of my life. My wife was furious that I hadn't just handed over the credit card. We were both terrified, having no idea whether the Secret Service would be back later in the night to search the house or simply haul me off to jail.

"If they come back," she said, "you know what they'll find."

I had grown increasingly dependent on marijuana, relying on it as the source of my creativity and inspiration, even as it had led me to take wilder and wilder risks. Now I had a young family, the Secret Service was on my doorstep, and I wanted to hold on to the weed even more than the credit card.

"I can't get rid of that," I said. "You don't know what you're asking."

"You have to get rid of it," she insisted. "Either the drugs go or I do."

Did she say that? In my head, at least, she said that. Somehow I had the clarity to see that this was a moment of truth. If I continued with my drinking and drugs, it would ultimately be the end of my marriage, my family, and—as the Secret Service agent said—my home.

Inside, I was at war with myself. I wanted so desperately to be free of my addictions, yet I did not have the courage to give up these things I loved so much. I was furious with my wife, American Express, and the U.S. government. *They* put me in this position of hopelessness and despair. *They* were responsible!

I was nearly in tears when I finally snapped. "FINE!" I shouted. "If I'm throwing *that* away, then I'm also throwing away all the liquor!" It was the kind of all-or-nothing thinking that is common with alcoholics, but in this case it saved my life. I furiously grabbed bottles from cabinets, throwing them into boxes and loading them into the car.

That's how I found myself in an alley behind my local supermarket, throwing away a thousand dollars' worth of perfectly good liquor into a dumpster.

I can't explain how difficult this was. It was the Friday night of a long holiday weekend, and while everyone else was starting the partying, all I could think was *I will never have fun again.* The thought was so painful that I had to redirect my mind, with great effort, from thinking about the long-term consequences of what I was doing.

I should really be giving this away to someone, my mind would think as I tossed in champagne from my wedding, bottles of grappa bought in Italy, and French wines I had been saving for a special occasion (like Thursday). The temptation to keep a few bottles to "give to a friend" was overwhelming, but I kept redirecting my mind, just focusing on throwing in the next bottle, and the next bottle, until all that was left was the marijuana.

I got back in the car and drove around town for a while, trying to summon the courage. *Think of all the good times we've had with this drug,* my mind told me. *Think of all the crazy, hilarious ideas it's given us. Think of facing life all alone, without its warm, comforting haze.*

I finally pulled into an empty parking lot and gazed at a trash can. Maybe if I could redirect my mind to the *physical movement* of throwing away the drugs, I could get through this. No long-term implications, just the *muscle movement* of tossing the bag into the trash.

One moment at a time, I walked step by step to the trash can. My mind tried to stop me, but I kept redirecting it to the next moment, the next moment, and the next. With an overwhelming pang of sadness and loss, I threw the drugs away, *my precious* lost to the fires of Mount Doom.

I didn't realize it at the time, but that technique of "redirecting the mind" was my first "mind hack." It was a technique I would use over and over again in the following months as I struggled to stay sober. Over time, I developed a catalog of these mind hacks, slowly reprogramming my craving for mind-altering *drugs* with mind-altering *mental habits*.

Just as it took some time to really see the transformation of my mind, it took some complicated legal wrangling before I finally gave up Barack Obama's credit card. It seems crazy now that I didn't just hand it over immediately, but it shows how we can become blind to our own insane thought patterns. The agents sitting in my living room were just a symptom of my bad thinking; the real problem ran much deeper.

Now I'm just incredibly grateful for that experience, because it not only changed my mind, it changed everything. I have come to have incredible respect and gratitude for the Secret Service. Never mind protecting the president: the way I see it, the Secret Service saved *me*.

Reprogramming My Mind

The first few months of sobriety were unbearable, and so was I. Every day was a roulette wheel of emotion: I could be furious, anxious, sulky, moody, or depressed, often simultaneously. One thought, however, slowly began to sprout a little bud of hope. *What if there was a way to reprogram my mind?*

Programming is in my blood. One of my earliest memories was my father taking me to visit the computer lab at the university where he worked. In my mind, the college's mainframe computer stood illuminated by a shaft of divine light, with a choir of angelic voices. In reality, it was probably fluorescent light and the whir of industrial air-conditioning units. But the effect on me was no less profound: somehow, that moment implanted a little seedling of geek into my tender eight-year-old uterus. Please don't ask me why I had a uterus.

My father approached the resident computer programmer, a heavyset man with a large, walrus-like mustache. "Ronald, this is John," my father introduced me.

"Hey." Ronald looked down at me, tape reels spinning in the background. (I might be mixing up some details of this story with a series of TV commercials for Control Data Institute.) "What can I do for you?"

"Can you create a punch card with John's name on it?" my father asked.

"Sure." Ronald handed me a card, a little larger than an index card, with small rectangular holes punched out. It was mind-blowing to stand in that computer lab among those massive, mysterious machines that required a swimming pool of coolant to keep them from overheating. I had the distinct feeling that *in here was another world*. I've since lost the punch card, but I'll never lose that memory.

When the cost of your own computer—*your very own computer!*—finally became affordable, I would pore over computer catalogs like earlier generations of kids would fantasize about Red Ryder BB Guns. I drooled over the latest machines with sexy names like TRS-80 and TI-99/4A, the pages of my catalogs stuck together with saliva and nerd sweat. I begged, cajoled, and badgered my parents until they finally bought me the legendary Commodore 64, the computer that changed my life.

They didn't just buy me a computer, they let me *keep it in my room*. There I began programming with a vengeance. There wasn't much to do in my hometown, so I immersed myself in the secret language of computers, teaching myself the basics: flowcharts, algorithms, variables, loops. I was lucky

enough to get in the first programming class taught at my middle school, and
by the end of the semester I was teaching the teachers.

Details are sketchy on when I lost my virginity, but I distinctly remember when I made my first computer hookup. I had just bought a modem for my Commodore 64, and I dialed into a friend's computer—one of the few people in my town who also had a modem (or who knew what a modem was). At first, there was nothing but a blank screen. I waited, not knowing what to expect. Slowly, the following letters appeared across my screen:

```
> Can you see this?
```

With that, the back of my head exploded. Here was my friend, across town, typing into his computer and having it *instantly appear in my room*. It was one of those transformative moments—my own version of Samuel Morse's first telegraph message. "What hath God wrought?"

At that moment, I realized THERE WAS A WAY OUT. Growing up in a small town, without much to do, I suddenly understood *my modem was a portal into another world*. I could communicate with other people, no matter where they were, in a strange digital world, which somehow existed alongside the physical world. But, unlike the physical world, the digital world gave me new powers, and I had the profound realization that *we could master these powers*.

After college, I landed a job at Ziff Davis, the world's largest computer magazine publisher, just as the Digital Revolution hit. I remember the first time I sent an email, the first time I saw the Internet, the first time I published a web page. Each time there was a feeling of incomprehensible joy that *the world is so much bigger and cooler than I imagined*—a feeling that continues to grow and expand to this day.

Because I grew up viewing the world through this lens of world-expanding technology, when it came time to get sober, it seemed natural to view my mind as a kind of computer. It struck me that a lot of the feelings and thoughts I was experiencing were like Adobe products: powerful, but riddled with bugs.

Could I reprogram my mind? Could I hack into the source code and change the way my mind worked? Was there an algorithm for recovery? I began to look for "mind hacks," techniques to identify and reprogram my problem thinking. I scoured textbooks of psychology, neuroscience, and computer science. I immersed myself in the latest research. I collected techniques from the greatest minds in history, from Albert Einstein to Benjamin Franklin to Nikola Tesla.

My goal was to create a formula, a collection of specific exercises—things I could *do* and *measure*—that would allow me to debug my problem thinking, then write powerful new code to rocket my life into exciting new orbits. As I practiced these mental exercises day after day, I found that not only was I staying sober but *my mind was getting better.* Like the world-expanding moments I had experienced with technology, my mind *itself* was expanding, and so was my life.

Years later, I come to you with a powerful message of hope. Not only have I become healthy, wealthy, and wise, but I have become *friends with my own mind.* I am happily married, a successful entrepreneur, surrounded by amazing friends. My life is rich in every sense of that word, and growing richer by the day. I want to share with you what I've found.

Think of the problems you're facing in your life—whether that's work, finances, health, relationships, kids—and reflect on how much time you spend *thinking* about them. If you hate that sense of obsessive worry and anxious doubt, then mind hacking is for you. You'll learn how to debug the negative thought loops that are keeping you stuck, to untangle your spaghetti mess of thinking.

Alternately, think of your goals and dreams, whether they are finding happiness, building relationships, achieving success, growing rich, or mastering the game of life (actual life, not the board game). Mind hacking teaches you how all these things begin in your mind and how you can reprogram your thinking to get there, to soak up the best things that life has to offer.

This is not just a book about overcoming addiction; it's a book about overcoming your *mental limitations*. You're about to learn powerful techniques that can help you accomplish anything you can imagine, whether that's losing weight, changing habits, starting a business, finding love, or building wealth. Your mind holds incredible untapped potential; get ready to learn how to unlock it.

Welcome to mind hacking.

<WHAT IS MIND HACKING?>

Hacker: "A person who enjoys learning the details of programming systems and how to stretch their capabilities, as opposed to most users who prefer to learn only the minimum necessary."

—The Hacker's Dictionary[1]

One of the greatest moments in computer history occurred, as it so often does, in an ordinary office cubicle.

Steve Wozniak was working late. After clocking out of his day job at Hewlett-Packard, he would often stay into the night to work on a secret side project. It was the mid-1970s, and he and his buddy Steve Jobs had recently been inspired by a demonstration of the Altair 8800, a build-it-yourself computer kit aimed at hobbyists. They had the radical idea that they could offer a similar computer *already built*. The user would still need to add a keyboard, video display, and a case—but the motherboard would be fully assembled and ready to crunch.

That computer, which would later be known as the Apple I, was the project that Wozniak was working on whenever he could find a spare moment. To finance their invention, Wozniak had sold his beloved HP-65 calculator, and Jobs his treasured Volkswagen Bus. Of the two, Wozniak was the technical genius, so into the night he toiled, long after his coworkers had gone home, in pursuit of this groundbreaking computer.

One night he hooked up a keyboard and a video display to his prototype, and something amazing happened: *it worked*.

"I typed a few keys on the keyboard and I was shocked!" he remembered. "The letters were displayed on the screen. It was the first time in history anyone had typed a character on a keyboard and seen it show up on their computer's screen right in front of them."[2] Today, we're surrounded by screens, so it is difficult to capture what must have felt like magic to Wozniak. It was like opening a portal to another dimension, discovering an entire world that *we had the power to manipulate*.

I sometimes still have that same sense of wonder and excitement when I'm using computers, even while doing something as ordinary as typing this paragraph. How is it that I can punch a cluster of plastic keys and have these words show up on a glowing screen? How can I speak into a phone and instantly have access to the complete store of human knowledge? How can I swipe my finger and launch a ham into orbit?

For the first time in history, we humans live in two worlds: the *physical world* of objects, and the *digital world* of websites, apps, and video games. We may still call the physical world "the real world," but that's just a figure of speech: the digital world is no less "real" than the physical world, just different.

Similarly, our *mental* world is no less "real" than the physical world, just different. Computers have given us an excellent model for thinking about the mind. Our thoughts are like bits: they're transient, ephemeral, invisible. And with some basic tools, they can be manipulated to do new and amazing things, an epiphany like Woz had in his cubicle all those years ago.

Mind hacking is like hooking up a keyboard to your head.

The Early Hackers

"Most of our generation scorned computers as the embodiment of centralized control. But a tiny contingent—later called hackers—embraced computers and set about transforming them into tools of liberation. That turned out to be the true royal road to the future."

—Stewart Brand, writer and hacker[3]

If you were a computer user in the 1970s, there's a good chance you were a hacker.

Hackers flourished on the campuses of schools like MIT and Stanford as well as hundreds of defense contracting companies and research laboratories around the world. They were as obsessed with learning as they were unconcerned with hygiene. Hackers were often solitary creatures, typing with pizza stained fingers at unfathomable speeds.

They might have been lonely, but they weren't alone. In the early days, hackers communicated through a high-speed global network known as ARPANET, an early precursor to the Internet. This strange new medium let them exchange ideas, information, jargon, and jokes; it was a creative, collaborative community of like-minded geeks.

"Hacking" was a badge of honor. It meant you not only loved technology, you understood how to *use* it to innovate and explore. You could write new programs by manipulating lines of obscure code; you could build your own motherboard; you could make a computer do something no one had imagined before.

As their numbers grew, hackers became a tribe, complete with their own language, values, and humor. As the tribe grew, so did its power. ARPANET eventually became the Internet, which transformed every aspect of modern life: education, government, finance, sex, even our view of the world. After the smoke clears, historians will agree the Digital Revolution made the Renaissance look like a picnic lunch.

And it was all started by hackers.

Today, a similar revolution is beginning, one that takes place not on keyboards and screens but entirely in your mind. Like the Digital Revolution, which couldn't be "seen" but was profound in its impact, this revolution is a silent meteorite hurtling toward Earth, a massive shift in human thinking. Just as the early hackers overturned the world with technology, *mind hackers are overturning the world of thought.*

Principle #1: Mind Hacking Is Free

"To be a hacker, one had to accept the philosophy that writing a software program was only the beginning. **Improving** a program was the true test of a hacker's skills."

—Sam Williams, *Free as in Freedom:*
Richard Stallman's Crusade for Free Software[4]

If there is one man in the world who does not get enough credit for his contribution to society, it is Richard Stallman.

Stallman deserves to be up there with Charles Babbage and Alan Turing and all those other stars in the geek constellation. A complex and controversial character, Richard Stallman has influenced your life and the technologies that you use, in profound ways.

And the thing that set Stallman off on his history-altering crusade was a *printer jam.*

In 1977, Stallman was a programmer at MIT's Artificial Intelligence Lab. Whenever he wanted to print a document from his workstation, he had to send the print job to the shared printer, which was located on another floor. After trudging up the stairs, Stallman would often find the printer was jammed, stuck in the middle of someone else's fifty-page print job. He'd clear out the paper jam, then babysit the machine until it jammed again. This would happen over and over, and then the printer would run out of paper.

The brilliant twenty-seven-year-old had recently graduated from Har-

vard, where he had quickly become a fixture in the hacker community. As he
stood over the printer, stewing over another paper jam, he began to approach
the problem like a hacker. He couldn't keep the printer from jamming, but he
could motivate his coworkers to clear the jams.

Rushing back to his desk, he cracked open the source code of the printer
program and came up with a brilliant hack. Who would be the most motivated to clear out a paper jam? *Someone waiting to print a document.* So whenever the printer jammed, he instructed the central computer to send out this
alert to everyone waiting for something to print:

```
> The printer is jammed, please fix it.
```

By sending the alert to people with waiting print jobs, he crowdsourced the
solution (before that was even a word). The solution was simple and elegant,
and it worked . . . until the day the new printer arrived.

The new laser printer was donated by Xerox's PARC lab, the research
and development unit responsible for world-changing innovations like the
graphical user interface, Ethernet, and the personal computer. But in this
case Xerox made one world-changing mistake: *they refused to release the source
code to the printer program.* This meant Stallman couldn't reprogram it. Now,
when the inevitable paper jams occurred, Stallman was back to banging his
head on the printer, his blood slowly boiling as each excruciatingly slow (but
laser-crisp) page was excreted from the printer.

Most of us can relate to the scene in *Office Space* where the three geeks
take a printer out into a field for a gangland-style execution. Small technology annoyances can build up over time until one day your rage explodes
and you find yourself in a field with a baseball bat, your hands stained with
toner.

So you can understand why Stallman tracked down the programmer of
the printer software, who had now taken a job at Carnegie Mellon, then flew
out to visit him. Stallman asked in a friendly way, hacker to hacker, if he
could have a copy of the source code. The programmer refused.

Something inside Stallman snapped.

"I was so angry I couldn't think of a way to express it," Stallman recalled later. "So I just turned away and walked out without another word."[5] To Stallman, it was a betrayal of the hacker ethic, a violation of the shared code that everyone should share code.

This started what can only be called a holy war. Stallman became an outspoken activist that all software should be free to use, study, distribute, and modify. He began publishing manifestos,[6] started the Free Software Foundation, and invented a new alternative to copyright called "copyleft." His revolutionary idea was that software with a "copyleft" license could be freely modified and copied, *as long as the resulting software was also free.*

In other words, programmers could rest assured that the work they put into improving software—like hacking a solution to the printer jam problem—would forever benefit the world, not be locked up and patented by some bloated software corporation.

Stallman's "copyleft" license, and later variants of it, had world-changing effects. It spawned GNU and Linux, which currently run a third of all web servers.[7] It gave rise to Apache, which is used by over half the servers in the world.[8] It birthed Firefox, which is used by a quarter of all people on the Web.[9] PuTTY. GIMP. Bugzilla. Thunderbird. Bitcoin. You could list literally thousands of projects, millions of developers, and billions of users benefiting from open source software.

And it all started in Richard Stallman's mind.

The mind hacking movement is free. It's called mind hacking, not Mind Hacking®, because we all own it. The online version of this book is under a Creative Commons (copyleft) license, available for free.[10] The tools and techniques you'll learn in this book are also free, which means they can be copied, modified, and improved.

Like open source software, together we are inventing *a science of self-improvement.* Our goal is to be able to say with a high degree of confidence, "If you do X, then you can expect result Y," tested and retested with hundreds of thousands of volunteers. These should not be vague and nebulous instructions like "Think positively" but specific things you can *do*. And they should work for the majority of people who put in the effort to actually do them.

Stallman didn't know how to fix the printer, so he found a hack that let him work around that limitation. Mind hacking should have that same spirit of creative problem solving. It should let the majority of us hack our minds via the simple, elegant solutions dreamed up by smart people like you.

Principle #2: Mind Hacking Is Experimental (and You Are the Experiment)

Seth Roberts, like so many of us, had acne.

Before he became the emeritus professor of psychology at UC Berkeley, a respected scientist, and a best-selling author, Seth Roberts had zits. His dermatologist prescribed the antibiotic pill tetracycline, a typical acne treatment at the time. Roberts was a grad student studying experimental psychology, so as practice for his class he began experimenting on *himself.* He varied his daily dosage of tetracycline, from zero to six pills, then wrote down the number of pimples on his face each day.

To his surprise, he found the dosage of his medication made absolutely no difference.

One day Roberts ran low on tetracycline pills, so he tried an over-the-counter benzoyl peroxide cream instead. To his surprise, the number of pimples decreased. When he stopped using the benzoyl peroxide cream, more pimples. When he started back up, fewer pimples.

This simple self-experimentation showed him that tetracycline didn't work for his acne, and benzoyl peroxide did. He learned something that his dermatologist, the "expert," didn't know. (Later research studies would show that certain types of acne are antibiotic-resistant, but of course Roberts already knew that.)

"My experience has shown that improve-your-life self-experimentation is remarkably powerful," wrote Roberts in Tim Ferriss's masterpiece of self-experimentation, *The 4-Hour Body*. "I wasn't an expert in anything I studied . . . but I repeatedly found useful cause-and-effect relationships that the experts had missed."[11]

The exercises you'll read in this book can be done on yourself: in fact, the *only* way to prove they work for you is through **experimenting on yourself**. By working together, mind hackers can also *pool* our self-experiments. We can show, through millions of personal tests, what works for the majority of us, making the program even better. You benefit from all the mind hackers who have gone before you—and you in turn help the generation to come. By helping stress-test this system, you reduce your own stress.

Because the mind is such an intimate, personal experience, you are the *only* person who can determine if it works for you. The nature of the mind means that you *can't* take someone else's word for it; you have to discover it yourself. You're the scientist, and your mind is the experiment.

Principle #3: Mind Hacking Is Mastery

Think back to the beginning of your geekhood. Whatever your geek obsession, whether you're into computers or comics or candle making, try to capture that feeling of first discovering the thing you loved so much. You probably weren't being paid to learn it; you were just learning it because you couldn't help yourself.

It was intrinsically fascinating and intellectually stimulating. But more than that, there was a feeling of what I can only call *joyful power* in conquering everything there was to know about that subject.

If you had to put that feeling into one word, it was probably "mastery."

In Daniel H. Pink's *Drive: The Surprising Truth About What Motivates Us*, he argues that mastery is one of the great motivators of human achievement.[12] This is why we spend hours detailing our maps of Middle-earth or memorizing a complicated riff on the ukulele. No one is paying us: the satisfaction of mastery is greater than any monetary reward.

The one thing that defines geeks is that we want to conquer a tiny piece of the world. We turn our death-ray intellects on a small subset of the world, desiring to possess it utterly, whether that is hand-forging a battle-axe for the Renaissance faire, folding the world's largest origami crane, or learning all the lyrics to *The Music Man*. We want to bring order to chaos, to control the uncontrollable.

In a word: *mastery*.

To master your mind is to master your life. There is no more worthwhile pursuit. As satisfying as it is to find 100 percent of the hidden weapons in your favorite video game, or to commit to memory lengthy poems in Klingon, if a fraction of that time can be spent mastering your mind instead, you will have a master key that can unlock all doors.

Approaching your mind with that same geeky mix of curiosity and craving, that spirit of conquering and completion, is what mind hackers are after. Remember that feeling; it is your fuel. As Nerdist founder Chris Hardwick has advised in his excellent book *The Nerdist Way*, see if you can take your laser-like powers of geek focus and train them on your own mind.[13]

Mind hacking is free. Mind hacking is experimental. Mind hacking is mastery.

We've learned the ground rules. Now let's learn how to hack.

Hello, World!

It's 2:00 p.m. on a cloudy November afternoon, and nearly one hundred developers are furiously typing on laptops at the Microsoft complex in Cambridge, Massachusetts. A large table is covered with energy drinks, coffee, and half-eaten pasta, the evidence of a massive all-night coding session. One of the developers is blowing a straw over a circuit board, trying to play "Mary Had a Little Lamb" on a makeshift electric harmonica. Another group is holed up in a conference room in front of a massive LED grid, which pulses in time to a techno beat.

This is the annual Music Hack Day, a twenty-four-hour "hackathon" to build something cool related to technology and music. The goal of a hackathon is to "pitch, program, and present"[14] a working app within an incredibly short window of time—say, twenty-four hours. Teams pitch their ideas to an enthusiastic crowd, pull an all-night coding marathon to get it finished, then demo their final software product the following afternoon. Unlike the typical software development cycle that can take months, hackathons cram all that innovation and problem solving into one caffeine-fueled blur of excitement.

By 3:00 it's time for the demos to start in the main conference room. There are sixty teams, so each group gets exactly two minutes to present. The first team shows off a stringed instrument made of yarn, which plays pre-recorded samples when you pluck the strings. Another shows an app called Hipstars, which analyzes your music tastes and gives you a one-through-five hipster rating. One group shows off a demo called Entrance Music that senses when you enter a room, then cues a computer to play your own customized theme song. The demos are creative, weird, and entertaining—*and they were built in twenty-four hours.*

How do they do it?

Talking about the "right way" to hack is like talking about the "right way" to play jazz piano, or write a novel, or raise a child. Hacking is a blend of creative and technical skills, an art and a science. There is an overall *process*, however, that we can talk about in three broad categories.

- **Analyzing.** We look at an existing piece of technology and figure out how it works. If we're hacking a remote control, for example, we might learn all about its programming codes or circuitry. Along the way, we identify problems or bugs and think of a way around them.

- **Imagining.** Creativity is at the core of hacking, ideally with an attitude of fun and playfulness. We imagine something new, some unexpected use for the thing: *Could that remote control lift a toilet seat up and down?*

- **Reprogramming.** We repurpose the technology to create the thing we've imagined. We write the code, solder the circuit board, duct tape the hovercraft. Through skill, iteration, and persistence, we make the idea a reality. (Behold, the remote-controlled toilet seat!)

In mind hacking, we take the same approach, **analyzing** the "source code" of the mind, **imagining** how cool it would be to make it do something else, then **reprogramming** the code with determined persistence until we see our lives transformed.

This book, then, is organized into three parts—Analyzing, Imagining, and Reprogramming—with do-it-yourself "Mind Games" to help you learn each set of skills. I *highly encourage* you to play the Mind Games and to keep track of your daily data in the practice sheet at the end of this book, or via the app at www.mindhacki.ng. This is how you monitor your progress and prove to yourself the program is working. Like a scientist, *write down your results.*

Not only will writing things down help you learn mind hacking, but multiple studies have shown it will help you *feel better.*[15] In one experiment, people who had recently lost their jobs spent a few minutes each day writing their thoughts and feelings about the layoff in a personal journal. After a few weeks, not only did test subjects experience improved physical and psychological well-being, but they were rehired significantly faster than those who did not write.[16]

When we think of great explorers like Columbus, Vespucci, and Cousteau, we hold them up as courageous heroes who conquered the globe. But now the outer world has been discovered; the next phase is *inward,* into the mysterious and fathomless reaches of our own minds. Those of us exploring our own mental potential are the next generation of explorers—and the best part is, *you can join us.* But, like these explorers, you have to draw a map. (Magellan didn't go anywhere without a pencil.)

The time has come to decide.

Your Moment of Truth

There is a tradition among geeks, when learning a new programming language, to start by creating a simple one-line program that displays the words:

```
> Hello, World!
```

Not only is this an easy first step to learning a new language, it also represents a sort of happy birth into the new environment. If you really want to learn mind hacking (and not just read about it), then I challenge you now to build up your desire, overcome your inertia, and take this critical first step!

MIND GAME

Accepting the Quest

Turn to the practice sheet at the end of this book. Write today's date, followed by "Hello, World!"

Decide on a *specific time and place* you will practice mind hacking each day, and keep the book in that spot to record your daily data.

You can also download the app at www.mindhacki.ng for daily reminders and community support.

The print edition of this book has two powerful benefits. First, you can write directly in the practice sheet—and I hope you will, since it's paper, *and paper was invented for writing*. Second, the book itself can serve as a visual prompt for your daily practice.

I recommend leaving *Mind Hacking* next to your bed. Each night, record the results of your daily practice in the back of the book. Each morning, *as soon as you get up*, the book will serve as a visual reminder to start your practice again. The physical book is designed to help you create this virtuous circle, a self-reinforcing loop that moves you forward.

Similarly, the practice sheet is designed as a twenty-one-day plan, an easy-to-follow framework that will cement your mind hacking skills, transform your thinking, and change your life. It's fine to miss a day here or there, but you will get maximum benefit from mind hacking if you complete the entire sheet. If you're serious about becoming a mind hacker, then make that commitment to achieve 100 percent completion.

Casual readers can still benefit from the book by picking up specific techniques that you can try out on your own thinking. For those hacking hobbyists, you can find a Quick Reference list of mind hacks at the end of the book. If you find them useful, then I encourage you to reread the book and complete the full twenty-one-day program.

Along the way, make it a point to *teach what you're learning to other people*. Share your mind hacks with others! The Roman philosopher Seneca said, "While we teach, we learn," and educators have long known the best way to lock in your own understanding of a topic is to teach it to someone else. Explaining these concepts to other people will not only help them, it will help *you*, because you will be able to articulate your understanding more clearly.

Ultimately, mind hacking is a great experiment that you can test for yourself. In fact, the only way to verify that mind hacking works is to *try it on your own mind*. The testing environment is yourself, and you are the ultimate proof.

Now, let's get hacking!

<YOU ARE NOT YOUR MIND>

"When people look at it . . . it looks crazy. That's a very natural thing. Sometimes when we look at it, it looks crazy. It is the result of reasoned, engineering thought. But it still looks crazy."

—Adam Steltzner, NASA engineer

On August 5, 2012, the engineers at NASA endured seven minutes of adrenaline-pumping terror.

They were monitoring the descent of *Curiosity*, a robotic rover the size of a car, as it landed on the surface of Mars. Hanging in the balance—and in the Martian atmosphere—was years of effort, the reputation of the agency, and $2.5 billion of research money.[1] The NASA control room was eerily silent, a high-stakes gamble on the engineering talent of everyone in the room.

The lead engineer, Adam Steltzner, represented a new breed of that talent. With pierced ears, snake-skin boots, and an Elvis haircut,[2] he looked more like a rocker than an engineer. He had overseen the complicated entry, descent, and landing sequence, in which *Curiosity* would have to brake from 13,000 miles an hour to zero in a perfect, tightly coordinated landing—all under its own automatic guidance systems.

Steltzner was also media-savvy, creating a short film before *Curiosity*'s descent, in which he explained the seven minutes of terror. "From the top of the atmosphere down to the surface," he explained, "it takes us seven minutes. It takes fourteen minutes or so for the signal from the spacecraft to make it to Earth; that's how far Mars is away from us. So, when we first get word that we've touched the top of the atmosphere, the vehicle has been alive, *or dead*, on the surface, for at least seven minutes."[3]

During that seven minutes, *Curiosity*'s heat shields would burn up to 1,600 degrees Fahrenheit. Its parachute would deploy, withstanding 65,000 pounds of force and slowing the descent to 200 miles per hour. Then the rover would cut the parachute and start the rockets, first diverting the rover away from the parachute, then looking for its targeted landing spot, a deep crater next to a 3.5-mile-high mountain.

Because the rockets would kick up a blinding dust cloud, they were attached to a "bridle," or platform, that would stabilize about 65 feet above the surface of Mars, then lower the rover down gently, tethered by a long robotic umbilical cord. The rockets would then cut themselves free, shoot themselves out of the way, and *Curiosity* would phone home.

Or not.

Steltzner and his team, along with geeks all over the world, held their breath. For seven excruciating minutes, long rows of blue-shirted engineers at NASA's Jet Propulsion Laboratory monitored the data on a seven-minute space/time delay.

Suddenly the entire room erupted in applause and celebration. Engineers leapt out of their seats, hugging each other, taking off their glasses, and wiping their balding heads. They were laughing, whooping, and hollering. *Curiosity* had landed safely.

Over the official broadcast, the mission controller was also shouting for joy. After a few moments he regained his composure. When you watch the video, you can still hear the excitement in his voice as he speaks the words: "It's time to see where *Curiosity* will take us."

In the ensuing years *Curiosity* has done extensive biological, chemical, and geological exploration of the planet. It has discovered that Mars may have once supported microbial life.[4] It is even preparing the way for human exploration of Mars.[5] All this controlled by its human masters from their command center back on Earth.

In a weird way, *you* are a kind of rover—not on Mars but on Earth. Instead of cameras and thermometers, your sensory data comes in via eyes, ears, nose, mouth, and skin. Like *Curiosity*, you are able to process this data through a layer of software called your "mind." Through this mind, you are able to direct specific commands, as NASA engineers are able to direct *Curiosity*: "raise arm," "practice banjo," "execute perfect three-point parking maneuver."

Imagine for a moment that you are the one controlling *Curiosity* via a high-tech, virtual-reality control room. Your eyesight is wired to its Martian cameras, your muscle movements control its robotic arms and sensors, your very thought propels its motorized treads along the planet's rocky surface. In a sense, that's what's happening right now, in the Earth rover that is your body.

But if the mind is the software layer, then who's controlling the mind? Who's the Adam Steltzner of your mind, the one who engineered it in the first place?

You are.

You Are Not Your Mind

This is the message I want to shout from the rooftops: *You are not your mind!*

Close your eyes and think about your own mind for just a moment. The fact that you can observe your mind, and think about it objectively, shows there is a "mind," and then an "observer of the mind," which we'll call "you."

In other words, you can separate "your mind" (which you have just pictured) with "you" (the one who is doing the picturing).

Got it? You've probably got it. But this idea is so fundamental to mind hacking, and yet so foreign to our everyday *experience*, that I will illustrate it via several different analogies. These analogies will serve as handy tools for peeling away "you" from "your mind," which a mind hacker must be able to do at will.

If you're a movie geek like me, perhaps you've had the experience of deconstructing a movie as you're watching it. It's the opening credits of *The Lord of the Rings*, and you're watching the title sequence, analyzing the music. Now comes the first scene, and you're evaluating the actors, admiring the cinematography, imagining the director orchestrating the action. And then . . . if it's a good movie, you quickly get *lost* in it, losing your perspective. You forget to analyze the movie, because *you're in it*.

Your mind is like that movie. Just as in the movie theater there is "you" watching a "movie," in your own head there is "you" watching your "mind." And like a great piece of cinema, you are absorbed in the movie of your mind: the thoughts, emotions, memories served up in a constant stream.

But the mind is no ordinary movie. It's a 3-D IMAX, Oculus Rift, full-on Sensurround-with-THX epic beamed directly into your head. And it's been *playing since birth*. So it's no wonder that we're so accustomed to watching it. It's a lifetime habit, and no one's ever told us, "Hey, you're watching a movie." Instead, they've told us, "*This is reality.*"

I sometimes picture a virtual reality mask that you pull on, with the headphones and goggles, but also with electrodes that tape to your forehead, beaming thoughts and emotions directly into your brain. After twenty, thirty, forty years of living that way, how would you even remember that you're in a simulation?

This is why it is so difficult for us to "pull ourselves out of the movie" for very long. If you think it's tough to run out of the movie theater to take a bathroom break, just try stopping the mind movie. In fact, just try *being aware* that you're watching a mind movie. Yet, being aware of this mind movie is the first step to mind hacking: we must learn to **analyze** the mind, with all its amazing cinematography, before we can hack it.

MIND GAME

What Was My Mind Just Thinking?

For the rest of the day, start building up awareness of your mind by asking yourself, as frequently as possible, "What was my mind just thinking?"[6]

    Keep track of how many times you remember to "check in" on your mind. At the end of the day, record your final score in the practice sheet at the end of the book.

A Diet of the Mind

The brilliant mathematician John Nash, who is the subject of the Hollywood movie *A Beautiful Mind* (as well as the book of the same name), is what the experts call "really good at math." He won the 1994 Nobel Prize in Economics for his work in the field of strategic decision making known as "game theory," and his work is used today in everything from artificial intelligence to military strategy.

Nash also suffered from paranoid schizophrenia. While his mental illness developed over many years, it was not until he was due to be promoted at MIT that his full-blown symptoms erupted. (He told the head of a rival department that he would not be able to accept the position because "I am scheduled to become the emperor of Antarctica.")[7] As his illness deepened, he spent time in and out of various mental institutions, suffering from "dream-like delusional hypotheses"[8] such as being persecuted by the federal government, aliens trying to contact him through the *New York Times*,[9] and the conviction that he was the Messiah.

What happened next is even more remarkable. Without the aid of medication, he gradually retrained his thinking using what he called a "diet of the mind." [10] In other words, he was still tempted by the delusional patterns, but he intentionally rejected them. He describes it as an ongoing habit of choosing the right thoughts, more "like a continuous process rather than waking up from a dream." This mastery of his mind—this ability to *disengage from his own mental movie*—led to tremendous career success later in life, including the John von Neumann Theory Prize, the Nobel Prize, [11] and the 2001 Academy Award for Best Picture (he should get credit for that one, too).

You are not your mind.

This is easiest to observe during "mental downtime," like driving or doing the dishes. When you're doing things that don't require a lot of concentration, your mind goes into overdrive, using those spare CPU cycles for projecting the movie.

Sometimes the movie is a feel-good family comedy: funny memories, pleasant thoughts, hopeful dreams. In these times, you see why the mind can be our best friend.

Sometimes the movie is a depressing English period drama: melancholy thoughts of despair, depression, or hopelessness, often involving tuberculosis. In these times, you see how our mind can be our worst enemy.

Your mind spends most of its time projecting into the future (plans, dreams, fears), or reminiscing about the past (memories, regrets, nostalgia). Frequently clips from the same movies play over and over:

```
> "Why did I say that? I'm such an idiot."
> "I don't know why I even try. I will never be able to do
  it."
> "If I don't watch every penny, I'll end up in poverty."
> "Does he really love me? Even though we've been together
  for so long, I'm still not sure."
> "My kids are going to get injured, I just know it."
> "Everyone at work is talking about me behind my back."
```

> "I hate him! I hate him! I hate him!"

> "This funeral would be a lot more fun if I were high."

We can all add our own mental movie clips to this list. It's difficult to reason with these kinds of habitual thoughts; they seem to just appear from out of nowhere. That's the way the mind movie works. Later, we'll learn how to begin directing this movie. For now, just try to become aware that you're watching it.

User vs. Superuser

Anyone who's spent time on a computer network has seen an error message like this:

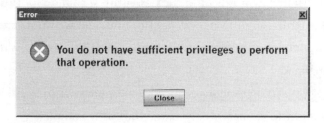

Which really means:

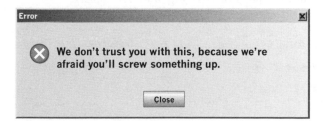

In simple computer systems, everyone has access to everything. But quickly this becomes unwieldy and dangerous: if you give a typical user access to the entire customer database, before you know it, he's accidentally erased 10 million names. ("Sorry, I was just cleaning my keyboard.") It reduces problems if people have access only to what they need.

Typically, the people who know what they're doing will maintain what we'll call "superuser" access, making sure the ordinary "users" have limited power. You can't view everyone's email account, only your own—but superusers can. You can't see everyone's files in the cloud, only your own—but superusers can.

This is why computer hackers always want to have superuser access. We call this "root" access or "rooting," because you're at the *root* of the system. This is where the power is. Root in, and everything is at your command.

As a teenager, I used to attend a monthly computer club where dozens of computer enthusiasts would meet up to pirate thousands of dollars' worth of computer software while eating Hostess Zingers. (Ironically, this early version of The Pirate Bay was held in the basement of a church.) This was long before the Internet, so software was hard to find, and we would spend hours copying programs on 5¼″ floppy disks until our drives would overheat; then we'd trudge home.

One night a stranger showed up. He said he was visiting from California, and he did look surprisingly tanned and fit, completely out of place among our pale, neck-bearded folk. He sidled over to me and asked, "What you got?"

I went through my entire list of games. "*Jumpman.*"

"Got it."

"*M.U.L.E.,*" I responded. "*Space Taxi. Zork I. Zork II. Zork III.*"

"Keep going."

"*Zork Zero.*"

"Anything else?"

It was crazy. *No one* had all those games. "How about *Pogo Joe?*"

"*Pogo Joe?*" He lit up. "I'll take it."

As we were copying the game, he asked, "You have *Blue?*"

"I've never heard of it."

"Check it out." He pulled out a disk with a piece of masking tape across the top. One word was written on it: BLUE.

"What's that?" I asked.

"It lets you make free phone calls."

In the days before digital phone systems, the legendary "blue box" was a piece of hardware that simulated a tone made by the phone company's analog switching relays, allowing you to make long-distance phone calls for free. (Before they invented Apple Computer, in fact, Steve Jobs and Steve Wozniak got their start building and selling blue boxes; one of Wozniak's original blue boxes is enshrined at the Computer History Museum.)

Blue was a software-only blue box: you called the phone company's information line, then held your phone receiver up to the computer speaker. *Blue* would blast out the magical 2600 Hz tone, putting you into "superuser" mode.

As it happened, I lived in Ohio and was dating a girl in Nebraska (if that doesn't prove my geek cred, I don't know what does). Once I got *Blue*, I went insane with long-distance phone calls. I was untouchable! I spent an entire month in blissful superuser mode, calling her multiple times a day for free . . . until my dad got the phone bill.

"SIXTY-THREE DOLLARS IN INFORMATION CALLS?" he screamed. I still remember him waving the phone bill in the air, as well as the exact amount of the bill. "SIXTY-THREE DOLLARS?" Apparently *Blue* wasn't *completely* free: you still had to dial up the information line, which cost fifty cents per call. I had made *one hundred and twenty-six information calls* in one month.

"Blue boxing" is similar to the concept of mind hacking: we are trying to log out of our usual "user" mode and log back in as "superuser" to unlock special powers and features. We're trying to trace our mental system back to its roots, where we can alter the code that controls our life.

Easy to understand, difficult to do. It's as if the mind, like an insecure IT overlord, wants to keep us locked in "user" mode. Even when we manage to get into superuser mode temporarily, before we know it, we're locked out. We realize that somehow we've slipped back into regular user mode, caught up in the content of the mind again. We've slipped back into the movie.

A fascinating study published in *Frontiers in Human Neuroscience*[12] shows that practicing this superuser mode can greatly improve our powers of "cognitive control," or the ability to focus our mind—which is linked to success in school, work, and life.[13] In the study, subjects were trained to focus on a specific target, to notice when their minds had wandered, then to return their attention back to the target. With practice, they were able to sustain attention and ignore distractions for progressively longer periods of time—actually *rewiring their neural circuitry to be more efficient*. (You'll learn this technique shortly.)

Put another way, the test subjects practiced getting into superuser mode, noticing when they were logged out, then finding their way back to superuser mode. As you'll soon see, getting logged out of the system is not the problem; the problem is *noticing* that you've been logged out of the system. In other words, the trick is becoming *conscious* of when you're in control of the mind (superuser mode) and when you're lost in the mind (user mode).

The takeaway is that, with time and training, you can learn to stay in superuser mode for longer periods of time. More important, you can learn to "interrupt" the usual user mode so you can quickly switch into superuser mode with a quick CTRL-M. If the "mind movie" idea doesn't appeal to you, think about getting superuser access to your mind instead.

Thinking vs. Metathinking

In junior high school, I was on the chess team: it was the only sport I could play without getting winded. My father taught me the basics of chess, and I joined the team understanding how all the pieces moved, as well as the basic concept of the game.

Our chess coach was also the school guidance counselor, giving him double geek credentials. I first met him during the summer, where he gave me a thirty-page, badly Xeroxed packet of chess *strategy*: all the openings, tactics, and endgames that you could use to win. I spent the summer squinting at this arcane document as scholars once studied the Dead Sea Scrolls, learning terms like "en passant" and "Ruy Lopez."

I gradually came to understand there was another level of playing chess— a *higher* level—where you focused on not just moving individual pieces to achieve the short-term objective of taking enemy pieces. Instead, you orchestrated the movement of *all* your pieces against your opponent's weaknesses in order to checkmate the king.

What my chess coach taught me was "metachess." He taught me how to work *on* my game, not just work *in* the game.

*Work **on** your mind, not just **in** your mind.*

Our modern word "meta" comes from the Greek preposition *meta*, which means "after." (Aristotle's *Metaphysics* was simply the book that came after *Physics*.) In the twentieth century, the prefix evolved into a term meaning "about its own category," or "an X about X"—for example, a "metatheorem" is a theorem about theorems in general. We use this prefix all the time in modern technology, such as metadata (data that describes other data) or metatags (HTML tags that describe the content of the HTML page itself). We even use it as an adjective, saying "That's meta" to describe concepts such as:

- Superman reading his own comic book

- Gödel's incompleteness theorems, mathematical proofs showing that mathematics can never be fully proven[14]

- Movies like *The Grand Budapest Hotel*, which is a movie about a girl reading a book written by an author who was told a story

- TV shows that break the fourth wall, like the *Doctor Who* episode entitled "The Mind Robber," in which the Doctor and his companions face the threat of becoming fictional characters

- Metaemotion (for example, being sad about being sad, or "We have nothing to fear but fear itself.")

- Metaprogramming, or programs that write new code for themselves at runtime; a simple example is the JavaScript eval() statement

- A metajoke, such as: "A priest, a rabbi, and a minister walk into a bar. The bartender says, 'What is this, some kind of joke?'"

Meta is, in fact, a sign of the times. We are gradually becoming capable, perhaps even *evolving* in our capability, of seeing things from the "meta" perspective. There is something transcendent and wonderful about this ability to analyze a thing from a higher level of abstraction, as if we are stepping into the next dimension.

In mind hacking, we are not just thinking: we are metathinking, or thinking *about* our thinking. The technical term for this is "metacognition." We are analyzing how our thoughts form, the sequence of thoughts that follow each other, how those thoughts drive our emotions and actions, and how they ultimately impact our lives.

Thinking is good! Thinking is how we make decisions, get stuff done, and move our lives forward. It is right to spend most of our time in thinking mode (and too few people do even that). But *metathinking* is the critical skill to develop for mind hacking. Ultimately, we want to become proficient at moving between these two modes.

Three Models, One Idea

So now we have three useful models: the "mind movie," "superuser mode," and "metathinking." These are three ways to think about one simple idea:

viewing the mind objectively, not getting caught up in content. In other words, *becoming aware of your own mind.*

As I was getting sober, I cannot remember a specific moment where I became aware of my mind; it was a dawning realization, a skill I gradually developed through the exercises in the following chapters. But as that awareness grew, so did a sense of freedom and excitement. I had identified so strongly with my mind that I believed everything it told me. Now I realized that *I had a choice.*

At this point, you also have a choice. While you are certainly aware of your mind, the challenge in mind hacking is to *increase* your powers of awareness. From here on out, I encourage you to approach your mind with a spirit of openness and curiosity. Observe it. Imagine how it could be used differently. In other words, approach your mind like a hacker.

Learning to develop this awareness, to *make it a habit*, is the foundation of mind hacking. As we learn to recognize what is the mind and what is "us," we can begin to observe how untamed the mind really is, as we'll see in the next chapter.

<YOUR MIND HAS A MIND OF ITS OWN>

Our minds are like misbehaving dogs.

When my wife and I were dating, she had a fifty-pound German shepherd that was, to put it politely, insane. The dog's name was Cassie, and while Cassie was supposedly *purebred*, she may have actually been *inbred*. We never asked questions about her family history; all we knew was that somehow Cassie's DNA double-helix got wrapped around the central strand like a leash around a pole.

Cassie was unpredictable, exhausting, and dangerous. When the doorbell rang, she would greet visitors by jumping on top of them full force, barking, slobbering uncontrollably, and sometimes biting them. At night, she would fall into a deep slumber underneath a coffee table, only to suddenly bolt upright at 3:00 a.m., overturning furniture and everything on it.

Taking Cassie for a walk was a daily adventure. First, you'd have to get the leash on, chasing her through the house as she knocked over chairs and appliances. Once outside, you'd hang on for dear life as she lunged randomly at any object that caught her attention: fire hydrants, balloons, invisible phantoms. She would slam her head into trees and occasionally try to attack children. If we had brought in the Dog Whisperer, he would have become the Dog Screamer.

Eventually, Cassie was taken away to live on a farm. We thought she needed a little more room to run. Apparently, we were right, because as soon as her new owners let her off their truck, Cassie went bounding off into the sunset, barking wildly. They never saw her again.

Our minds are like that dog, constantly chasing squirrels, mailmen, and passing cars. This is easily observed by simply trying to quiet your mind. Within a few minutes your dog mind will leap up, run around in circles, and pee on the carpet. It doesn't want to sit still, and it doesn't want to obey your commands. What's more, the temptation to *let the mind do this* is incredibly overwhelming.

I'm going to sit quietly and keep my mind empty, you vow to yourself. After about thirty seconds of silence, your mind starts whimpering. *What did you eat for breakfast?* it asks you. *Cornflakes, right?*

I'm sitting quietly, you say, swatting at the dog mind with a rolled-up newspaper.

How do they make cornflakes, anyway? it barks. *Where's the corn?*

In any other situation, this question would hold zero interest for you. But now it becomes a burning obsession. *How* do *they make cornflakes?* you find yourself asking. Then: *No! We are sitting still, dog mind!*

The mind settles down for a second, then jumps back up, barking louder. *There's a rooster on the front of the cornflakes box! What's that about?*

That's when the dog takes off, with you running behind it on a leash. Before you realize what's happened, you've listed your top ten favorite breakfast cereals, created a new recipe for bacon muffins, and mentally replayed a grade school argument about Pop-Tarts.

It's as if our minds have been misbehaving for so long that we've tuned out the incessant barking and are content to live with the craziness. In fact, we seem to *relish* the craziness, to take comfort in the stream of thoughts. I can't emphasize enough how seductive and irresistible our thoughts can be, especially when we're trying not to get lost in them. It is incredibly easy to get caught up in the movie—and when we're caught up in it, we're not directing it.

Now for the good news: like dogs, *our minds can be trained.* And, like a well-trained dog, our minds can go from a holy terror to man's best friend. If you've ever owned a well-behaved dog, you know the pleasure of having a faithful companion, an obedient helper, and a loyal pal—and your mind can be the same way. (Sorry, cat people. Find your own analogy.)

Truly, your mind can be both your worst enemy *and* your best friend.

The Attention Economy

Imagine that you wake up tomorrow in a parallel universe. Everything in this universe is the same except for one big difference: *money has been replaced by attention.* All citizens have little meters attached to their heads, right between the eyes, that show where they've been spending their limited daily supply of attention.

Let's say, in this universe, a minute of your attention is worth a dollar. This means when you sit down and enjoy a couple of hours of TV, you're paying $120 for the privilege. Spending a few minutes (and you really are "spending" a few minutes) catching up with friends will cost you $10. When you drive down the interstate, you're leaking pennies and nickels whenever a billboard catches your eye.

When your mind obsesses over some difficult relationship or unfortunate event, you pay $15 or $30 at a time. Over the course of a week, this adds up; you might spend a significant portion of your monthly attention on anxiety and guilt. In this universe, most citizens have no idea where all their attention goes; it just seems to get used up, and there's never enough to go around. Everyone, it seems, has attention deficit disorder.

This is because there are hidden "attention taxes" everywhere you look: all kinds of messages, alerts, and interruptions that slowly drain your focus. Someone sends you a text message, and you pay a quarter for the ensuing conversation. You spend hundreds of dollars a year sifting through unwanted email. You happily spend thousands of dollars watching advertisements on TV. Your attention is constantly being depleted without your knowledge.

In this universe, instead of hiring a financial advisor, you hire an attention advisor. Looking at your forehead meter, he shows you how to stop the attention leaks and how to reduce your attention tax. Then he teaches you an incredibly valuable trick. When you focus your attention *on attention itself*, it's like putting money in a savings account with compounding interest. He cites the old proverb "It takes attention to make attention," showing you how to invest attention to create even more of it.

Now for the twist: except for the forehead meter, *you're in that universe right now*.

The idea of an "attention economy," named by Babson College professor and management consultant Thomas H. Davenport, states that human attention, *not money*, is the scarce and valuable commodity.[1] All those Super Bowl advertisers are paying for all that human attention. Times Square is such valuable real estate because it attracts so much attention. A tech company with millions of users can be worth billions of dollars, even if it doesn't make a dime in profit, because of its attention-generating power.

Time is money. And *your* time—in the form of your attention—is your most valuable resource.

The Myth of Multitasking

I know someone who multitasks during his one-hour commute to and from work each day. I don't mean he just sends text messages or checks his email. I mean he actually watches movies on his laptop while he's driving. Or he'll pull up the *New York Times* on his tablet and put it on the steering wheel so he can read while he drives. Sometimes he'll play games. He gets in a lot of accidents.

Go to any technology conference, and you'll notice that practically everyone is immersed in a screen—phone, tablet, laptop—paying little attention to what is actually going on. It's disconcerting to speak at these events, because *no one is looking at you.* Everyone is "listening with one ear," which seems worse than not listening at all. These are conferences that cost thousands of dollars to attend, and people are barely paying attention!

Or take a look in the conference rooms of companies across the world, where there are dozens of employees supposedly engaged in the meeting but actually lost in their screens. If everyone is only giving the meeting one-tenth of their attention, it requires ten people to make up the attention of one person. This is why so many inessential people are invited to the meeting: hopefully *someone* is listening, someone who can make the critical decision!

We pay an awful lot of attention tax through the digital distractions that tempt us every waking moment: email, websites, instant messaging, social media, text messages, and funny photos of overweight babies. Who can resist all these things? And why would you *want* to, when clearly they are put there for our enjoyment?

> *Those who multitask*
> *Are doing nothing fast.*

The torrent of information, as well as the technologies that feed it to us, are so new that we don't have rules for them yet. We indiscriminately install time-wasting apps, leave on concentration-interrupting alerts, and jump at text messages, emails, and friend requests. If our minds are already misbehaving dogs, then these technology toys are like squirrels in the front yard.

The problem is not the technology but our indiscriminate and undisciplined use of it. These attention-grabbing apps and alerts quickly become bad habits, making our minds even less disciplined. Just as we must watch our diet to avoid getting fat, we must watch our *attention-interrupting habits* so that our mental powers do not become weak and flabby.

Among the worst of these habits is multitasking. There is a wealth of scientific research indicating that "multitasking" really means "doing several things badly at once." Multiple studies have shown that you're slower when you switch between tasks than when you do one task repeatedly[2]—and that you grow less and less efficient as the tasks grow increasingly complex.[3]

Psychiatrist Edward Hallowell defines "multitasking" as a "mythical activity in which people believe they can perform two or more tasks simultaneously as effectively as one."[4] And we continue to buy into the myth that multitasking is possible, and even desirable. We keep open a chat window so we're always "available." We jump at text messages. We keep a feed or news ticker running so we're "plugged in" or "connected."

Stanford University sociologist Clifford Nass, one of the pioneers of multitasking research, explained it like this:

> People who multitask all the time can't filter out irrelevancy. They can't manage a working memory. They're chronically distracted. They're even terrible at multitasking. When we ask them to multitask, they're actually worse at it. So they're pretty much mental wrecks.[5]

In other words, this fragmentation of attention is making our minds weaker, not stronger. Each distraction you allow yourself actually makes you *less* productive, *less* capable, and *less* . . . SQUIRREL!

Sorry, thought I saw a squirrel.

We All Have ADD

If multitasking is so bad for us, why do we keep at it?

Because it is *addictive*.

As you wait in line at a restaurant, do you pull out your phone? As you're getting ready for bed, do you check your email one last time? As you're sitting at a table, *with flesh and blood human beings*, do you interact with humans somewhere else? It's this addictive nature of our devices that has led writer Soren Gordhamer to ask: *Are we in control of technology, or is technology controlling us?*[6]

MIND GAME

Squirrel!

For the rest of the day, try to become aware of whenever your attention is pulled away from the task at hand by either digital or human interruptions. Try to become aware of the feeling of "broken flow" when you lose your concentration.

Keep track of how many interruptions you notice. At the end of the day, write down the final number on your practice sheet.

Is it any wonder attention deficit disorder is so prevalent? Although ADD was first described in 1902, it has been steadily on the rise in recent years. Now, according to the U.S. Centers for Disease Control and Prevention, nearly 10 percent of U.S. school-age children (ages four to seventeen) have ADD—to say nothing of the *adults*.[7]

Here's an easy way to see the mind clearly: occasionally go into a meeting or social gathering without your device, and *be aware of your impulse* to check a screen. You may find screen checking has become an ingrained habit, a *compulsion*—and the only way to begin correcting this impulse, this *addiction*, is to first become aware of it. This need to constantly check a screen is a symptom of the misbehaving dog mind, as is the need to have several browser tabs open, to do homework while watching TV, or to simultaneously play three hands of online poker while flying a plane.

Your mind craves information; that's what it eats. Unfortunately, your mind has bulimia.

A 2013 study from Kent State University surveyed five hundred students and found that higher smartphone use was highly correlated with higher anxiety: stress and screens go hand in hand.[8] Another study at the University of Worcester in Britain found the same holds true for workers: the more they check their smartphones, the more they suffer from stress, "because people get caught up in compulsively checking for new messages, alerts and updates."[9]

The great Russian physiologist Ivan Pavlov trained dogs by always ringing a bell before he presented them with food. Eventually he found the dogs would slobber uncontrollably as soon as he rang the bell, *even before he had presented the food*: their bodies had become "conditioned" to prepare for food when the bell was rung. Similarly, attention-interrupting "tools" like email alerts and instant messaging have conditioned our minds to expect a tiny burst of informational pleasure.

Let's say you get a text message alert. (Maybe it even sounds like a bell!) You know there is new information waiting for you: it might be someone saying hello, it might be a picture of your sister's kids, it might even be an exciting emergency. That bell has *conditioned* our dog minds to slobber with anticipation as we stop whatever we're doing and tend to the text message. We are all Pavlov's dogs.

Try to become aware of the precise feeling, so you can recognize it when it happens. Try to capture that feeling of discontinuity, the "jerkiness" of being pulled out of concentration. That drug-like cycle, the addictive temptation with its accompanying mini-burst of pleasure, is what we want to overcome. The disobedient dog thrives on this chaos; *it is a picture of mental weakness.*

Now, compare this with the feeling of "flow": being immersed in an activity, with unbroken concentration. You might call this being "in the zone" or "losing yourself." You can probably think of some activity where you're in the zone: making music, coding, or just reading a great book. Close your eyes and picture that flow of effortless concentration; try to get a sense of what it feels like. That's what the well-trained mind is all about. *This is a picture of mental strength.*

We can learn how to develop this state at will. The key to this retraining is the lost art of **concentration**, the subject of our next chapter. Concentration training brings clarity and focus to our mental efforts and is a foundational skill of mind hacking. It's not just about turning off your instant messenger but also about learning specific exercises that actively increase your powers of concentration. This is how you discipline the dog.

<DEVELOPING JEDI-LIKE CONCENTRATION>

You probably remember the scene from the original *Star Wars* where Luke Skywalker is learning to use the Force on board the *Millennium Falcon*.

"Remember, a Jedi can feel the Force *flowing* through him," Obi-Wan Kenobi instructs him as the training droid shoots Skywalker on the leg.

"Ha-ha!" mocks Han Solo. "Hokey religions and ancient weapons are no match for a good blaster at your side, kid."

"You don't believe in the Force, do you?" Luke asks him.

"There's no mystical energy field that controls *my* destiny," Solo snorts. "It's all a lot of simple tricks and nonsense."

"I suggest you try it again, Luke." Obi-Wan puts a helmet on Luke's head, blocking his vision.

Concentrating, this time Luke blocks the lasers, relying entirely on his instincts. (Solo never apologizes.)

Whether you are more like Obi-Wan Kenobi or

Han Solo when it comes to believing in the Force, you certainly know the power of concentration. A moment's reflection will probably show you that your best work, strongest ideas, and deepest insights come from moments of concentration, when your mind is calm, clear, and focused. You may even long for these moments and wish that you had more time for them.

In the sequel *The Empire Strikes Back*, Luke goes off to train with Yoda, developing incredible powers of concentration. Now he is able to stand on one hand upside down while balancing Yoda and levitating rocks. Han Solo and his blaster, meanwhile, get frozen in carbonite.

This chapter is your Jedi training.

Reclaiming and Retraining

The great psychologist William James once said that the skill of "voluntarily bringing back a wandering attention, over and over again, is the very root of judgment, character, and will. An education which should improve this faculty would be the education *par excellence*."[1] In the following pages, I will lay out that education, *par excellence* (which is French for "very good at golf").

It may help to think of your attention in two ways. First, you have what is called "voluntary" or "top-down" attention, which is where you choose to direct your mind.[2] Right now it is focused on these words. We don't have a good vocabulary for attention, so the best analogy I can give you is the proton pack from *Ghostbusters*, the concentrated energy guns they use to capture ghosts. That "stream" of positively charged energy is like your voluntary attention: you can point it at this, and this, and this. (Just, please, *don't cross the streams*.)

You also have a "reflexive" or "bottom-up" attention, which is when something "catches" your attention. Though sometimes this is exceedingly useful, such as when we hear someone call our name in the middle of a noisy public square, it is also what we might call "being distracted by shiny objects." METALLIC SQUIRREL!

The great challenge of our time is to strengthen our "top-down" attention (our ability to concentrate), while weakening our "reflexive" attention (our tendency to become distracted). Therefore, developing your powers of concentration involves two components: *reclaiming attention* through reducing distractions, and *retraining your mind* through concentration exercises.

Reclaiming attention Involves taking an inventory of all the *avoidable* distractions that surround you, then reducing or eliminating them. These are lifestyle changes, usually small and incremental, that add up to a huge difference over time, because they help keep you focused on a daily basis.

Retraining your concentration involves a specific set of Mind Games that will help you not only calm the mind but also harness its power. Your success with mind hacking will depend largely on how seriously you take these games and how deeply you integrate them into your lifestyle. Everything else builds on these games: they're your mental fundamentals.

These are not just one-time lessons but core life skills that will make you better at everything you do. If you're an entrepreneur or businessperson, these concentration games will give you an edge, a competitive advantage. If you're involved in a relationship or a parent of young children, they will bring you greater calm and mental clarity. They will bring you focus, poise, and confidence, and create a mental environment where you can train your mind to accomplish incredible achievements.

The exercises in this chapter are meant to become habits. If you're learning how to live a healthy lifestyle, you don't just do a month of ab crunches and then call it quits: you integrate exercise and movement into your everyday life. Similarly, the more you can work these skills into your daily routine, the more powerful you will become at mind hacking.

You may not learn how to levitate objects with your mind like Luke Skywalker, but you could very well develop a levitation technology, then license out the patent. Anything is possible!

Reclaiming Attention

The sixteen people gathered at the Dart NeuroScience Convention Center in San Diego have the best memories on the planet.

These "memory athletes," as they are known, are here to compete in head-to-head "memory battles." They stare at computer screens that rapidly flash names, numbers, or words. The athletes memorize these random lists with amazing speed, then recall them with pinpoint accuracy. The annual Extreme Memory Tournament, or XMT (also a great name for a memory drug), offers $60,000 in prize money to the winners.

My favorite competitor is Ola Kåre Risa of Norway, who wears not only sound-canceling headphones that you might see on a flight runway but a cap with a long visor and *side flaps*. His side flaps are hilarious, ensuring that no distractions enter his peripheral vision as he stares at the computer screen. He looks like a horse that's wearing blinders while landing a plane.

But there's science behind this approach. As Henry L. Roediger III, one of the psychologists studying these memory athletes, tells the *New York Times*, "We found that one of the biggest differences between memory athletes and the rest of us is in a cognitive ability that's not a direct measure of memory at all but of *attention*"[3] (my emphasis).

The fundamental skill these memory athletes have developed is known as "attentional control," or the ability to choose what to pay attention to and what to ignore. We might also call this your ability to *concentrate*.

Sometimes you'll say, "My attention was wandering," which is an excellent phrase that shows that you have something called an "attention," which is sometimes under your control but sometimes goes for a brief walk. This "attention," this focused point of consciousness, is under continual assault, much of it by the environment you create for yourself.

Some distractions cannot be avoided. If you work in an office, for example, your coworkers may be motorized disturbance makers. Unenlightened bosses may expect you to be available via chat twenty-four hours a day.

Parents, especially new parents, may find it especially challenging to focus, since young children are interruption machines. (My wife gave a name to her bewildered, sleep-deprived mental state when our kids were small: "mom brain.")

What we're targeting is the *unnecessary* distractions, the interruptions that we allow into our lives either out of habit, ignorance, or laziness. "We are easy to distract, and very bad at doing two or more things at the same time," says Columbia Law School professor Tim Wu. "Yet our computers, supposedly our servants, constantly distract us and ask us to process multiple streams of information at the same time. It can make you wonder, *Just who is in charge here?*" [4]

Getting rid of these distractions will make you happier, since your mind sees digital distractions as *unfinished tasks*. Productivity guru David Allen, the best-selling author of *Getting Things Done*, warns of the "mental clutter" of unfinished tasks, and there's research to back up his claim. In the 1960s, Russian psychologist Bluma Zeigarnik showed that starting any kind of task gives your mind a mild psychic anxiety until that task is complete. [5] Unfinished tasks nag at you.

Unwanted digital distractions add to that "mental clutter": each one reminds you there's another task needing your attention. Part of our Pavlovian response to jump at those notifications is the need to close that open task loop, to consider the project "complete," no matter how trivial ("Well, now I *have* to get my social media profile to 100 percent!"). Get rid of the notifications and you'll reduce your mental clutter—and your anxiety. More important, you'll be able to focus on what's more important.

- **Instant messaging.** If you're in the habit of messaging frequently throughout the day, *stop*. Uninstall IM apps or set them to "Away" by default. The problem with messaging is that distractions create more distractions: when you respond, another response comes back. In between, you are trying to get fragments of work done. It's a high-interruption environment.

- **Text messaging.** Just like instant messaging, text messages distract our concentration over a longer period of time because of the slow pace of a conversation carried out over text. Few of us are willing to turn off text messaging on our phones, but you *can* set aside times of the day to respond to messages, or wait until you're between tasks, rather than answering immediately.

- **Internet distractions.** Whether it's checking your stock portfolio or updating your fantasy football team, we pay heavy attention tax on Internet distractions. It's okay to allow yourself these distractions, but ideally as "rewards" for periods of focused concentration. By flipping the model on its head—using Internet distractions as rewards for *completing* difficult work, rather than *avoiding* it—you can greatly improve your concentration as well as your quality of work.

- **Audible and visual notifications.** App developers and software companies have a vested interest in *getting you to use their products*. Therefore, they have developed a wide array of attention-getting devices to remind you to check in—icons, messages, notifications, beeps, boops, and *ding-dong aroogah*s. Like Pavlov's dogs, these train us to expect a quick hit of satisfaction whenever the bell rings—so *turn off the bell*. Get the icons out of your system tray! Turn off notifications! Ruthlessly uninstall!

- **Media.** Do you switch on the TV as soon as you enter the house? Do you turn on a podcast as soon as you get in the car? We are voracious *consumers* of media, binge-viewing entire seasons of TV, watching sports games as we eat in restaurants, keeping "one eye on the TV" as we do our daily tasks. Instead of making media consumption your default activity, with brief periods of silence, try to make *silence* your default activity, with planned *entertainment breaks* of TV, radio, or movies. Silence is golden.

- **Email.** Eliminate! Filter! Unsubscribe! Do you really need the daily Doctor Who Digest, or the impassioned pleas to save the chickens in El Salvador? It's true that individual emails are easy to delete, but each mailing list you get *off* eliminates dozens of micro-distractions and deletions in the future. They add up.

To begin, you're only investing an hour in cleaning up these distractions. Set a timer, and stop when the hour is up. Don't fall into the ironic trap of wasting the next week trying to reclaim your time. You're not after perfection, just simplification; you can always continue to simplify later. In other words, *simplification is a process.* It's much better to start with an hour, then set a recurring appointment in your calendar to review and eliminate further once a month. Keep it simple, Skywalker.

MIND GAME

The One-Hour Investment

Spend one hour cleaning out or turning off unnecessary digital distractions, including:

- Instant messaging
- Text messaging
- Notifications and alerts
- Time-wasting Internet sites
- Unnecessary emails

Set a recurring appointment in your calendar for a monthly review to eliminate further.

Count the number of digital distractions you turned off, and record that number in your practice sheet.

Retraining Your Mind

"If you just sit and observe, you will see how restless your mind is. If you try to calm it, it only makes it worse, but over time it does calm, and when it does, there's room to hear more subtle things. You see so much more than you could see before. It's a discipline; you have to practice it."

—Steve Jobs[6]

The basic concentration game is simple—so simple, in fact, that you may be tempted to ignore or discount it. Some people call it "meditation" or "mindfulness," but I prefer to call it *concentration training*, since that's what it is. Your mind hacking success rests largely with the seriousness and tenacity with which you approach this basic game. Like chess, it offers a lifelong challenge of mastery.

- Find a comfortable place to sit where it's reasonably quiet and you're free from distractions.

- Sit with your legs crossed or your feet on the ground. If you find yourself getting drowsy, stand.

- Close your eyes and focus on your breath.

- Relax each part of your body, starting from the top of your head, your forehead, eyes, cheeks, mouth, jaw, etc., down through your toes, then back up again. This should take two to three minutes.

- Mentally tell your mind what you are going to do, e.g., *For the next twenty minutes, I will focus on the breath, so that I may develop superhuman concentration.*

- Now focus on the breath at the center of the nostrils.

- When you find yourself following your mind ("lost in the movie"), simply redirect it back to the breath at the nostrils. Score +1 point for noticing and calmly redirect back to your breath. (Keep track of your points on your fingers or in your head.)

- You can set a soft timer or alarm for twenty minutes, though eventually you will get a feel for when twenty minutes have passed.

- Remember to write down your final score (the number of times you caught your mind wandering) on your practice sheet.

Make it your goal to practice faithfully, and you will see the benefits. Studies show this type of game will improve attention,[7] regulate emotions,[8] keep you healthier,[9] make your relationships better,[10] and even make you feel good.[11] It's scientifically proven to nourish, revitalize, and refresh both you and your mind.

How to Make This a Habit

Practicing for twenty minutes a day is a terrific goal: just wake up half an hour earlier. If your schedule doesn't allow it, then do fifteen, ten, or even five minutes to start. The trick to succeeding over the long term is to make this concentration game a *habit*. As with getting your body in shape with regular physical exercise, getting your mind in shape requires developing a *routine* that integrates this exercise into your lifestyle.

In his book *The Power of Habit*, Pulitzer Prize–winning journalist Charles Duhigg proposes that we can more easily create new habits by "bookending" them with a *cue* to start the habit, as well as a *reward* once we've completed the habit.[12] For example, if we're trying to create a habit of daily exercise, we might always set our running shoes by the bed as a visual *cue* upon waking, and always treat ourselves to a post-workout smoothie *reward* when finished.

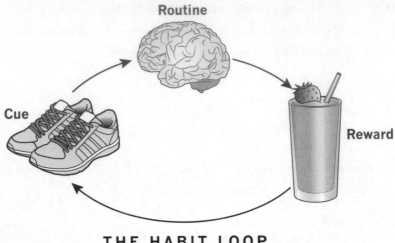

THE HABIT LOOP

In order to turn the concentration game into a positive habit, then, you need to consciously set up a *cue* to begin, as well as a *reward* when complete. Here are some tips:

- **Choose a consistent time.** First thing in the morning is best, before your to-do list kicks in. Make it a part of your day-starting routine, as I do, and be sure to *practice at the same time*.

- **Choose a consistent place.** Pick somewhere you will not be disturbed; this can be your bedroom or a spare room. I have been known to practice in my car before work (often while parked).

- **Choose a consistent reminder.** Keep this book by your bed, or set out your favorite chair. You can also set a digital reminder like a phone alert (here's where alerts can be a useful thing).

- **Choose a consistent reward.** The first reward is logging your score into your practice sheet, creating a positive feedback loop. Adding in a second healthy reward locks in that motivation: a shower, or breakfast, or music.

- **Be consistent** in your cue and reward. As with training children or pets, continuing to enforce the same routine, day after day, will help the practice habit stick.

- **Practice, not perfection.** Avoid all-or-nothing thinking, where you either stick to a perfect schedule or you don't practice at all. The important thing is to *keep practicing:* If you miss a few days, just pick it back up!

Variations [13]

There are many variations on the basic concentration game to keep it interesting, but my strong recommendation is to *decide beforehand which variation you will play*. The temptation will be to switch to a new variation mid-practice, which is a subtle trick your mind will play to amuse itself. Pick one and stick with it.

- **The Illuminati.** Instead of focusing on the nostrils, focus on the point between the eyebrows.

- **Alien Blaster.** Pretend each thought is an alien. Focus on your breath while remaining vigilant for stray aliens breaking through your defense shield. Whenever you see a thought arising, mentally say, *Thought*, which disintegrates the alien with a hydrogen-ion particle blaster.

- **The Third Nipple.** Instead of focusing on the nostrils, focus on the point between the breasts.

- **Golden Breath.** Instead of focusing on the nostrils, focus on the *air itself* as you inhale and exhale. Imagine that you are taking in pure oxygen, a delicious smell, or a healing elixir.

- **The Slow Jam.** Do the basic concentration game, but as you exhale, try to capture the "feel" of sinking into a warm bubble bath, relaxing into a sexy rhythm, or grooving to a slow jam.

- **Rise and Smile.** Perform any of the variations above, but smile while doing so. (See more on the scientific value of smiling in Section 3.2.)

There are also variations of this game that you can play during the day. In my experience, there's no substitute for dedicated concentration practice, but these are excellent mini-games to hone your concentration skills throughout the day. Count +1 awareness point each time you catch your mind wandering, and remember to get back into the game.

- **Single Threading.** Take any mundane activity, from walking the dog to tying your shoes, and "slow down" your thought process to focus on each moment of the experience: a "single thread" of attention on the task at hand.

- **Go with the Flow.** At any point throughout the day, become aware of the "flow" of sensory input flowing into your mind, the stream of unbroken thoughts and sensation. See how long you can observe the "flow" and not get lost in it.

- **The Proton Pack.** Pretend that you're a Ghostbuster and pay attention to the "stream" of your attention as it spews outward. Watch where you're aiming it and see how long you can visualize that stream. Busting makes you feel good.

As you play these concentration games, you may find that habitual thoughts, memories, or emotions keep popping up. You might even have deep insights or realizations about your life, your personality, or your childhood history. *This is normal.* What you are seeing is the areas that need to be reprogrammed. You're becoming aware of your own mental code.

The trick is to mentally note these things and tell your mind you will process them later. Avoid the temptation to get lost in another "mind movie." As if you were training a child, gently say to your mind, *That's interesting, but we're going to focus on the breath now*. After your practice, write down any insights or observations on your practice sheet. You can always discuss them with your therapist later.

Above all, try to be *gentle but firm* with your mind. You may get frustrated when you notice your mind wandering, but remember: the *act of noticing* is the very sign of progress! Resist the urge to get angry or impatient with yourself; this is just more mind movie. Develop the habit of completely letting it go. The attitude is one of nonresistance: Gently set the mind back on your object of concentration and begin again. This is why we call it "practice."

As we diligently practice these games, we develop clarity of mind and a sense of its underlying codebase. We also develop the *precision* necessary to analyze the code that runs our mind. This is the aspect of mind hacking we'll talk about next.

<DEBUGGING YOUR MENTAL LOOPS>

"You need to learn how to select your thoughts just the same way you select your clothes every day. This is a power you can cultivate. If you want to control things in your life so bad, work on the mind. That's the only thing you should be trying to control."

—Elizabeth Gilbert [1]

When personal computers first came on the scene, every department store had a computer section with the latest models on display: the Apple II, the Commodore 64, the Atari 800. Most of these computers came installed with BASIC, the language that allowed anyone to learn how to code.

As a young nerd, I had an expert level of BASIC (oxymoron), but I had a friend with almost zero knowledge. He knew how to write exactly *one* program. He was a bit of a prankster, and would have me watch out for salesclerks while he wrote his one program on all the computers in the store:

```
10 PRINT "I AM THE WORLD'S
GREATEST HACKER"
20 GOTO 10
```

Running this program would cause the computer to endlessly display the words "I AM THE WORLD'S GREATEST HACKER," an infinitely repeating testament to his mighty programming prowess.

My friend had mastered the loop, which is one of the essential building blocks of computer programming. When we're writing software, loops are how we get stuff done. More than that, loops help us get stuff done *efficiently*. Loops are a shortcut. Sure, we could write:

```
x=1;
x=2;
x=3;
x=4;
x=5;
```

until our program was 1,000 lines long and all we had done was count to 1,000. Or we could just write:

```
for(x=1;x<=1000;x++)
```

which accomplishes the same thing, in one elegant line of code.

We have *counting* loops, which run through a set of instructions a defined number of times ("For every row in this spreadsheet, apply this formatting"). We have *conditional* loops, which run through a set of instructions if certain criteria are true ("Each minute, check if the time is 12:00, and if it is, pop up an alert"). We have *infinite* loops, which even my friend understood.

The complexity of modern software is mind-boggling: layers upon layers of loops. Say you're reading this on an electronic device. The highest-level programming loops may tell your device what content to display and how to display it. Underneath that are loops running the reader app itself. Go deeper and you'll find loops controlling the operating system that runs the apps. Still lower are loops running the device itself: the battery, the clock, the screen. The layers build on top of each other, growing increasingly sophisticated, and increasingly *amazing*.

When you're using a word processor, making a phone call, or playing a video game, you don't notice the loops. The loops are forming a higher-level, abstract representation that seems utterly divorced from the programming going on behind the scenes. All the richly complex software that we take for granted is run on top of simple building blocks like loops. It's one of the most amazing things about computers . . . and our minds.

Our Minds Are Loopy

Like software, our minds are also programmed with loops.

Think back to how useless we were as babies. It's as if our parents got a new computer, except there was nothing installed on it, not even an operating system. Turn it on, and all they got was some low-level configuration menu that told the newborn how to suck, cry, and poop.

Over the next six months, we learned some basic skills: sensory input, rudimentary cause and effect, the beginning of language, and some simple emotions. Whether we discovered it through trial and error, parental guidance, or luck, this programming "stuck" through simple repetition, through practicing these fundamental skills over and over.

By the age of three, we had grown incredibly complex: walking, running, speaking in complete sentences, and expertly manipulating our parents. We now had a sophisticated operating system, which was *learning to program itself* through a continuous stream of questions. ("Why are clouds? Who are trees? Where is muffins?") All these skills, habits, and personality traits were reinforced by constant repetition: loops building on loops.

Over the years, we learned increasingly complicated mental loops. First we learned there were substances going in our mouth. Then we learned some of these substances tasted better than others. Later we learned these substances were called "food," and then we learned how to get more of the foods we liked.

Along the way, we were continually developing mental models—thought habits or loops—that saved us time later on: *I only like white foods. I usually get food after a boo-boo. Grandparents give better food than parents.* These loops optimized our behavior, making it more efficient to get what we wanted. Our code grew more elegant.

In school, we learned through repetition. First we learned the concept of numbers, then we learned operations on those numbers, then we learned layers of abstraction like algebra and trigonometry. And always the loops, in the form of practice, exercises, and tests. Later, these loops helped us with specific tasks like managing money, doing home renovation, and acquiring businesses. Our operating system was now fully formed, and specialized apps were beginning to appear.

Society deeply embedded its values into us through continued repetition and reinforcement: Sunday school, teen magazines, pop music, Disney movies, TV shows. And always the advertisements, repeated over and over, expertly crafted loops telling us what to buy. Pop-up ads and spyware were getting installed on our operating system, slowing everything down.

Perhaps the most powerful loops were the ones making up our self-image and our view of the world. If we came from a safe, stable home, we probably grew up to see the world as a safe and welcoming place, thanks to the power of that repeated daily experience, that repeated loop. If we came from a chaotic, broken home, with repeated instances of lying or abuse, the world became a disturbing, dishonest place.

If we were always told that we were brilliant, we grew up believing it.

Now, when we meet with difficulty or setbacks, our default response might be *Hey, I'm smart and I'll figure this out.* If we were constantly berated for how terrible we were, we grew up with that internal dialogue. Now, when we run into trouble, we think, *Just my luck. Another failed project.*

If our parents acted like money was always in short supply, our mental loops probably run something like *I've got to save every penny or I'll be broke,* even when we have plenty of money and such thoughts have far outlived their usefulness. If our parents spent money frivolously or gambled it away, our mental loops might go like *It's only money, and besides, I really need that rare albino giraffe.*

If our parents had a reasonably functional relationship, we may have internalized loops like *It's okay to compromise with your partner* or *We are working together as a team.* If they fought bitterly, even after they divorced, we may have deep programming that says *Long-term relationships do not work out* and *I am destined to live angry and alone.*

As with the low-level loops of code running the clock on your computer, these loops can be so deeply embedded that they're difficult to detect. They run everything, yet they're invisible. That's because, to a very great extent, these loops are *self-fulfilling prophecies*: if our loops tell us we're good with people, then we'll probably seek out opportunities to meet more people, and through simple practice we *will* be good with people. If our loops tell us we'll never amount to anything, we'll be nervous and afraid to jump on new opportunities, and we ultimately *won't* amount to much.

Addiction is a loop. We eat, or drink, or smoke, in order to feel better and better. We feel horrible the next morning, so we start the loop again, while our lives get worse and worse. Just about anything can be made into an obsessive loop: talking, pornography, flame wars, religion, worrying, shopping, sex.

Just as it's hard to believe that loops of code can build an immersive video game, it's hard to believe that our thoughts, our behavior, and even our *lives* could be built through loops. Once you begin to observe your mind closely, however, you'll find these mental loops control just about everything you do.

Your loops create your thoughts.

Your thoughts create your actions.

Your actions create your life.

Therefore, *the quality of our loops determines the quality of our lives.*

Fix your loops,

Fix your life.

This is great news: it means that even though many of our loops may be invisible to us, there is one simple way to find them, and that is by looking at *the quality of our lives.*

When you use a well-designed app, *it just works.* Think about your favorite search engine: how fast, powerful, and intuitive it is. Behind the scenes are millions of well-designed loops, all optimized to work together harmoniously.

Similarly, if our mental loops are reasonably well designed, our life *works.* We are successful at work, play, relationships, money, and love. Successful does not mean perfect; it simply means that our lives have a minimum of friction, a minimum of *pain*. Where there's pain (**outward** pain, such as a series of failed jobs or relationships, or **inward** pain, such as depression or anxiety), there's usually a faulty loop. In fact, pain is an excellent indicator that we need to *examine* our loops.

Thus, improving the quality of our mental loops involves tracking down the faulty thinking that is causing us pain. It's a process that is similar to tracking down faulty computer code, or **debugging**.

The First Computer Bug

If there were a Geek Hall of Fame, "Amazing" Grace Hopper would deserve a nomination.

In 1947, "Amazing" Grace Hopper was a forty-year-old computer programmer at Harvard University, working on the Harvard Mark II, a huge electromechanical computer that used relays, switches, and vacuum tubes to perform amazing feats like calculating square roots in about five seconds.[2]

One afternoon, Hopper and her team of engineers began a routine test of the machine's adding and multiplication functions, when they noticed something wrong. In those days everything was hardware, so you would manually inspect the computer itself—like inspecting a car or a washing machine—to see if a part had failed. The engineers removed the panels on the enormous machine one by one until finally they found the problem: a small moth had made its way into one of the relays.

For years, the word "bug" had been used informally by geeks to describe hardware malfunctions. Even the grandfather of geeks, Thomas Edison, had referred to faults and difficulties in his systems as "bugs."[3] So you can imagine the pleasure and delight of those Harvard Mark II engineers of *literally finding a bug* causing a bug. This was like winning the comedy lottery!

They reverently removed the moth from the relay, determined to enshrine this insect in the annals of computing history. They taped the moth into their daily logbook with the words "first actual case of a bug being found."[4]

Grace Hopper delighted in telling this story throughout her career, popularizing the use of the word "bug" to describe a system error or fault. She spent her later years on college lecture tours telling that story, along with many others from her amazing career in technology. She frequently stressed to young people the necessity of personal change. "I find in general that human beings are allergic to change," she would often say, explaining that innovation and open-mindedness give people the freedom to try new things.[5] In a sense, she argued for the debugging of the mind.

Decades after Hopper's death, bugs are a part of life for those of us who work with technology. We can all relate to a system crash, a computer freeze, or a life-sucking moment of doom where you lose the last four hours' worth of work—all thanks to bugs.

For those who develop software, bugs are a part of the process. *A program almost never works properly the first time*. You write some code, you run it, and it breaks. This is normal. This is part of the job. You track down the errors, or bugs, in your loops of code, then you rewrite the loops, and run it again. You do this again and again, hundreds or thousands of times, until you have a working prototype. Then you hand over your software to a team of beta testers. "Try to break it," you tell them.

By using the software in different and unexpected ways, your testers find more buggy loops, which you track down and correct. Some bugs are small: a misspelled word or a missing semicolon. Some bugs are huge: a gaping security hole or a navigation system failure.

Let's say my friend made one error when typing his brilliant program:

```
10 PRINT "I AM THE WORLD"S GREATEST HACKER"
20 GOTO 10
```

How long did it take you to spot it?

Yes, accidentally writing *a quotation mark instead of an apostrophe* would signal the *end* of our PRINT statement, causing the computer to choke on line 10. My friend would no longer be the world's greatest hacker; he would be the world's greatest SYNTAX ERROR.

This kind of bug is easy to track down, but many bugs are far more insidious and complex. Some can only be reproduced under specific circumstances or unusual situations—so unusual that the developers have great difficulty ever finding them. "Show me the steps to reproduce the problem" is a common refrain among programmers. "Well," says the person reporting the bug, "I was in this spreadsheet, and I clicked this menu item. Wait, maybe it was this other menu item. Hmm. Well, it crashed this morning, so please fix it before lunchtime."

Bugs Cause Pain

Years ago, my company used a well-known video editing application to produce online videos. For the sake of not being sued, we'll call this program VideoBug. Being a high-end video editor, VideoBug required an enormous amount of memory and computing power. It would *run* on a slower computer, just *not very well*. There was no way to know whether your computer was optimized for VideoBug until you found yourself hitting your head with a hammer out of sheer frustration. Using VideoBug was a great way of really coming to *deeply understand and appreciate* the pain of bugs.

Sometimes the pain would be subtle, like a split-second audio glitch that sounded correct in the preview video but only showed up in the final video. You'd render the video again and again, trying to get the audio right, missing deadlines, missing sleep, missing your child's first piano recital. Eventually you'd delete the entire video project, rebuild it from scratch, and twelve hours later it would work.

Sometimes the pain would be acute, like when the computer would hang after working on an all-night video project, taking all your effort with it. "Well, didn't you save your project?" someone would ask, and you'd silently vow to kill them, right after you slaughtered the entire VideoBug development team.

One day, one of our team members was in the other room, separated by a three-foot reinforced concrete wall, when I suddenly heard him explode with rage. It was terrifying and violent, with a torrent of screaming expletives and the sound of a massive filing cabinet full of CDs being pulled to the ground.

Freaking VideoBug, I thought to myself.

Now multiply our frustration times hundreds, thousands, or millions of users of the VideoBug software, and you see how seemingly small bugs can cause tremendous difficulty and frustration. To this day, a simple web search turns up thousands of user complaints about all the issues not listed on the official VideoBug website.

You may ask, "Why didn't you just get a video editor that works?" Eventually, we did. But we had so much experience with using VideoBug—we were so trained to save our project every ten seconds and expect frequent crashes—that it was easier *in the short term* to live with terrible software rather than learn a whole new system.

It's an appropriate metaphor for our minds. Our mental programming—our loops—can cause us pain, but it's often easier to just live with the pain than invest in learning a new system.

The rewards of learning the new system, though, are potentially *infinite*. Not only do our negative loops cause us pain, they hold us back. They limit us. If we switch to a new video editor, we'll simply make it easier to create videos. In the world of the mind, though, getting rid of our limitations unlocks anything we can imagine, because *imagination is at the core of mind hacking*.

How to Debug the Mind

To recap: our minds are the product of thousands of repeated lessons, good and bad, true and false, accurate and inaccurate. These have been ingrained as mental "loops" that can be positive (*I like to exercise*) or negative (*I will never find true love*). They can be constructive (*I should spend money responsibly*) or destructive (*I would be happier if I had a drink*).

These habitual thoughts control our emotions, our behaviors, and ultimately our lives. Because they are deeply embedded, the product of years of experience and upbringing, these loops can be hard to track down. The best way of debugging these negative loops is to look at the quality of your life, more specifically for areas of *pain*. For example:

- Difficulty in relationships
- Difficulty at work
- Difficulty with family members
- Legal trouble
- Money trouble
- Health trouble

- Persistent negative beliefs (*I'll never succeed. People are untrustworthy.*)

- Persistent negative feelings (cynicism, hopelessness, despair)

- Persistent failure

- Anxiety

- Depression

- Addiction

- Living in your parents' basement and/or your car

For me, being visited by the Secret Service, and the subsequent fallout, was an enormous pain point: a sign that something needed to be changed. But there were plenty of smaller pain points along the way, like getting caught sneaking vodka from the liquor cabinet by my father—*in my thirties.* And of course the everyday mental pain that was causing me to sneak vodka from the liquor cabinet in the first place.

The problem is that we can get so used to the pain that we become numb to it. Like a person who's always worn a pair of ill-fitting shoes, we can convince ourselves that it's not worth the trouble to change. *The pain isn't that bad,* we might rationalize, or *I can live with it.* Meanwhile, the pain gets worse, and we limp through life in size 4 loafers.

Fortunately, there are several methods we can use to uncover the loops that cause us this pain. The first is based on a Japanese management technique known as **The Five Whys.**

Method #1: The Five Whys

Sakichi Toyoda was, you might say, the king of Japanese geeks.

In the late 1800s, many Japanese textile factories still used wooden hand looms to produce cloth. They were labor-intensive, slow, and expensive. After several years of experimentation, Toyoda invented a steam-fueled power loom that quadrupled textile production, cut costs in half, and produced better quality cloth to boot.[6]

The success of the Toyoda power loom made Sakichi Toyoda a rich man, and he funneled that money into developing new inventions to make his looms even faster and more powerful. Automatic shuttle changers. Interchangeable parts. Eventually a fully automatic loom. Today he's known as "King of Japanese Inventors," the Asian Thomas Edison, and his story is taught to every Japanese schoolchild.

Toyoda's genius was not just around his inventions but also around his innovations in the *process* of manufacturing. To Toyoda, it was *processes* that failed, not *people*. When troubleshooting problems in his factories, he invented a technique known as the "Five Whys" to track a problem down to its root cause.

The technique is simple: when you encounter a problem in your factory, instead of beating the employee who's responsible, you step back and answer the question "Why?" five times until you get to the deeper issue.

Let's say you're an automobile manufacturer. One of your new car models has a problem: under certain conditions, the gas tank explodes. While the natural response is to figure out a short-term solution (replace the gas tank, recall the cars, deny the story, etc.), the Five Whys discipline seeks to find the root (or roots) of the problem.

What's the source of our exploding gas tanks?

1. We used a gas tank from a new supplier. *Why?*
2. Our old supplier could not deliver in time for production. *Why?*
3. Production was rushed to meet an accelerated schedule. *Why?*
4. Management wanted to accelerate the production schedule to impact end-of-year sales. *Why?*
5. Management bonuses are tied to annual sales.

By following this tree of "Why?" down to its roots, you can make changes that impact the entire system, that tackle the problem at the *source*, not at its *result.* Here, the result (exploding gas tanks) is just the surface of a much deeper problem (management gaming annual sales bonuses at the expense of safety). Problems usually manifest themselves far down the chain from where they started.

Note the "five" in "Five Whys" is somewhat arbitrary—it may take six whys, or four, to find the root problem. Usually, in fact, there are multiple roots to the problem, so you need to ask "Why?" down several divergent paths. The basic idea, however, is powerful: *Continue asking "Why?" until you get to the source (or sources) of the problem, and fix the problem there.*

Toyoda's "Five Whys" technique was eventually embraced by the entire manufacturing industry as a best practice, and ultimately found its way to the modern corporate world as well. The company he founded, Toyoda Automatic Loom Works, lives on as the Toyota Motor Corporation, which makes some of the highest-quality automobiles in the world.[7]

Now, let's look at Charlie, a twenty-five-year-old programmer who has a pattern of not being able to hold a job: either he gets fired, or he quits.

Why can't you hold a job, Charlie?

1. I can't get along with my bosses. *Why?*
2. Sometimes I'm insubordinate. *Why?*
3. Now that I think about it, it's more like I don't want to be forced to do something I don't believe in. *Why?*
4. Because I had to do that a lot growing up. I hated that my father was so dominating. *Why?*
5. Because it made me feel like I can't be trusted to make my own decisions.

Like stepping through a program to find the faulty code, we've debugged one of Charlie's negative thought loops—the hidden feeling that *I can't be trusted to make my own decisions*—that manifests itself as insubordination, which ultimately leads to the pain of being fired.

Let's take another example. Darla is a thirty-three-year-old mother of three who is afraid of walking alone at night:

1. I'm afraid of walking alone. *Why?*
2. I'm afraid someone's going to attack me, and no one will be there to help. *Why?*
3. My older brother often scared and threatened me, which left me with a feeling of never being safe. *Why?*
4. Because no one was there to protect me. My parents didn't take it seriously. They acted like I was overreacting, like I was the crazy one. And now I *feel* like the crazy one! *Why?*
5. Because I continually think that the world is not a safe place.

We've debugged a negative thought loop (*The world is not a safe place*) that can be reprogrammed with a positive thought loop (*I am safe in the world*). More on reprogramming in Section 2.4.

The goal of "Five Whys" is to keep the focus on *you*. Not on other people. Not on circumstances beyond your control. If you end up with an answer like *Because my husband is a moron* or *Because I was born with bad luck*, try again. Train your microscope on your own emotions, thoughts, and actions, and be ruthlessly honest with yourself.

Let's take one more example. Ed is a forty-five-year-old project manager who suffers from depression. It's not serious enough to seek professional help, but enough to impact his daily life. Two or three times a year, he cycles through a depression that feels like he is "swimming against a powerful current."

1. I've had these depressive episodes since I was a teenager. *Why?*
2. It feels like all the happiness of life is gone. *Why?*
3. Life seems hopeless, out of control. *Why?*
4. Depression runs in my family. My aunt had it, my grandmother had it. I sound a lot like my aunt, actually. It shows you how it runs in the family. *Why?*
5. Well, I guess it's just a part of me, who I am.

Aha! We've uncovered a problem loop (*I am a depressed person*) that is also a self-fulfilling prophecy. Because Ed sees himself as someone who goes through periodic cycles of depression, he becomes less likely to help himself when he feels a new episode coming on (say, by exercising or seeing a doctor). Thus, he *is* a periodically depressed person, caught in the buggy loop of bad thinking.

It's true there is probably a physiological component to his depression, but we're trying to get to the *problem thinking* that's contributing to the pain. Since thoughts create feelings,[8] focusing on the feelings can be a useful way of getting to the thoughts.

In fact, a great trigger for the "Five Whys" is when you notice a *persistent thought*. Instead of suffering through these anxious or depressing thoughts that won't seem to go away, see them as red warning lights flashing on Toyoda's assembly line. A persistent thought usually indicates a problem loop, and asking *Why is this thought so persistent?* as the first of your Five Whys can help you trace it back to its source.

By practicing the "Five Whys" on yourself, gently questioning each of your long-held beliefs, you can often find the root problem. If not, here's a second method.

Method #2: Worst-Case Scenario

Much of our mental pain is based on fears of imaginary events that simply will never happen. This fear is often just beneath the surface, gnawing away at us. By *exaggerating* the fear, we can pull it out into the open. We do this by asking one question: **What's the worst-case scenario?**

Let's take the case of Francine, a twenty-eight-year-old receptionist. She finds herself stewing over a parking attendant who overcharged her earlier in the day and who then refused to refund the money. She "catches" herself obsessing over this small event hours later and determines to root out the problem thought.

Francine is self-aware enough to know that she has problems spending money: she hadn't wanted to park in the garage in the first place. Spending money, especially *unnecessary* money, causes her anxiety.

So we ask her: What are you afraid of? What's the worst-case scenario?

The worst-case scenario is that I spend too much money and can't make enough to cover my expenses.

That's bad, but we're going for the absolutely worst case, so we encourage her to continue.

I lose my apartment. I can't afford food. I have to live in a shopping cart under a bridge.

And then?

I waste away and die a miserable death.

Actually, this isn't the *worst*-case scenario: that would involve an alien apocalypse, where the invaders keep her alive in an eternal state of unrelenting agony. But let's not get silly.

The point, though, is that Francine *will* see her fear as a bit silly. Even if she went broke, she could file for bankruptcy or turn to her parents or friends for support. She would be able to get government assistance long before she ended up under a bridge. Still, feelings are persistent, even when we logically understand they're silly.

So we take our fears to their extreme conclusions to *help us identify the limiting belief*. With greater clarity, Francine can now synthesize her thought loop into something like this:

It's dangerous to spend money, because I will die a miserable death.

Or simply:

It's dangerous to spend money.

In the next section, we'll talk about how Francine can reprogram her mind using positive loops like *It's safe to spend money* or, better yet, *I have plenty of money*. These new loops will eventually replace the old code and make Francine happier and more successful. She may still get angry with the parking attendant for overcharging her, but she'll be able to keep it in perspective: one parking ticket does not mean catching rats for food.

Let's take another example: Gary is a high school teacher in his early thirties who is looking for a partner. He had a date last night, which went well until he flubbed the good-bye by awkwardly going for a kiss, which went badly, as his date turned away at the last minute. He has been obsessing over this detail all day until he finally examines his thinking in an effort to get some relief.

What's the worst-case scenario?

The worst-case scenario is that she doesn't date me anymore. I really like her, and I will be crushed if she doesn't feel the same way.

Feeling crushed doesn't feel good, but this is nowhere near a worst-case scenario.

The worst-case scenario is that she never calls me back. This causes me to lose confidence, which women can detect immediately, and they start to become repelled by me. Eventually I give up completely and accept that I'm doomed to be completely alone. Worse yet, I live to be 108, outliving even my family and friends. So I die completely alone, with no one to hold my hand except the nursing home attendant who happens to be taking my blood pressure at the time.

Wow! At least Gary has an imagination. But if Gary looks closely at this story he's just told, he should start to detect the underlying belief:

I'm no good with women.

Gary has to be careful with choosing his positive thought loop. A simple reversal (*I'm good with women*) can seem boring in comparison to alternatives like *Women find me irresistible* or *I am magnetically sexy to women.* These new loops can have enormous consequences in the direction of Gary's life, so he must take great care when rewriting his mental code. More on this in Section 2, which we will get to shortly.

Method #3: Third-Person Perspective

A third method you can use to bring your dark thoughts into the light is taking the Third-Person Perspective. This method is as simple as asking yourself, *If this was someone else's problem, what would I say to that person?*

Take the case of Haley, a married mother of two who frequently worries for her children. Most parents worry, but Haley has made an art form out of it, insisting that her kids wear helmets when sledding and stay inside during the summer because of the threat of ticks and Lyme disease.

One day, sick from worrying about her son's report card, she decides to examine her thoughts. She imagines herself sitting across the kitchen table *from herself*, as if she were a friend. If she had to analyze the thought loop that was going through her friend's head, what would it be?

Probably that her kids will get sick, or injured. Or worse.

What's her problem loop?

The world is dangerous. But the world is dangerous!

What's her problem loop in regard to her kids?

My kids are not safe unless I'm watching over them every minute.

And can she watch over them every minute?

No. Especially as they get older.

And *should* she watch over them every minute?

Sometimes, but no.

So what's the positive equivalent of her negative thought loop?

My kids are safe.

How much better it feels to go through life thinking that your kids are fundamentally safe rather than expecting doom around every corner!

Now, it's true that sometimes our kids *do* get sick and injured, so it may feel inaccurate or wrong to think, *My kids are safe*, especially if you have a deeply ingrained loop of *My kids are not safe*. But isn't it *far more accurate* to believe that your kids are fundamentally safe than not safe? After all, most of us grow up okay, despite the inevitable sledding crashes and tick bites. For Haley, constantly repeating to herself *My kids are not safe* is simply not consistent with reality. It is a *projected* reality that Haley is capable of reprogramming herself.

When using the "Third-Person Perspective" technique, it may help you to imagine a friend sitting across the table, or it may help you to imagine a scientist, a great leader, or another trusted person of authority. In Napoleon Hill's classic success book *Think and Grow Rich*, he told of a technique he used for years that he called the "Invisible Counselors."

He first chose nine great men whose character he wished to emulate in his life: historical figures like Thomas Edison, Charles Darwin, and Ralph Waldo Emerson. Each night before he went to bed, he would close his eyes and imagine these legendary figures around a table with himself in charge as chairman of the group. He would often put his current problems before each of the characters, then ask his imaginary advisors to share their wisdom.

This was not just a problem-solving technique but a way that Hill used to rebuild his own character in the mold of these great men. Before addressing Abraham Lincoln, for example, he would butter him up by saying, "Mr. Lincoln, I desire to build into my own character the keen sense of justice, the untiring spirit of patience, the sense of humor, the human understanding, and the tolerance, which were your distinguishing characteristics."[9]

Night after night, Hill performed this mental exercise, and he found that each of the leaders began to develop his own personality. Lincoln would often arrive late, then walk around the table gravely with his hands clasped behind his back. Thomas Paine would often get in spirited arguments with the naturalist Luther Burbank. These imaginary meetings became *so* vivid that Hill temporarily discontinued them, concerned he would lose the ability to distinguish imagination from reality!

I've personally used the "Third-Person Perspective" to get help or advice from many of the geniuses you'll read about in this book. I don't believe I'm communicating telepathically or summoning the dead. I *do* believe, however, that a part of my mind already has the correct answer, and the "Third-Person Perspective" can be a useful way of logically tracing back my problem loop to its source so I can discover the answer for myself. Plus, it's fun to discuss your problems with Yoda.

Getting to Bare METAL

For true geeks, bare metal is even sexier than bare skin.

"Bare metal" is a term we use for a new piece of computer hardware with no operating system or even an assembler. It's just clean hardware with no layers of junk added in. Sometimes we'll talk about "programming on the bare metal," which is the incredibly technical work of developing these tools for a new computer. In the hierarchy of geekdom, developers who bit bash on bare metal are the highest-level (i.e., lowest-level) geeks around.

In mind hacking, we're approaching our minds with that same spirit of "getting to the bottom of things," or going for the root loops that are controlling our emotions, thoughts, and actions. In fact, METAL can be used as an acrostic for:

My
Emotion
Thought
Action
Loop

We've seen how everything we do is preceded by a thought, and that thought is often preceded by an emotion. By developing clarity of mind through regular concentration games, then using the debugging tools outlined in this section, we can track down the logical sequence of Emotion-Thought-Action that is causing problems in our lives. (You'll soon learn how to reprogram your METAL, but you can't fix the bugs until you identify them.)

On your pad of paper, after your daily concentration game, I recommend tracing My Emotion-Thought-Action Loop, using the debugging tools you've just learned. It might look something like this:

Emotion	Thought(s)	Action(s)
Anxiety about a new assignment at work	*I don't know if I can deliver this in a way that will make my boss happy.*	Doubting the results of my work, redoing the project multiple times, unnecessary overtime and stress
Depression about my relationship with my partner	*We're not as close as we were before, and we're drifting further apart.*	Getting angry at my partner over minor issues, passive-aggressive behavior, and frequent criticisms
Self-criticism over that stupid thing I said	*Why did I say that? Why did I say that? WHY DID I SAY THAT?*	Being self-conscious about everything I say to this person in the future
Regret about that decision I made in the past	*I shouldn't have done that. I wish I could go do it all over. My life would look so much better.*	Self-doubt and procrastination about making any decisions in the present
Worry about my career after graduation	*The job market is terrible. I have no experience. There are lots of other people more qualified than me.*	Reading gossip sites and watching funny llama videos instead of looking for a job

There's a strange kind of power from seeing your emotions, thoughts, and actions spelled out in words. Until you write them down, they will exist as swirls of feeling in your mind. Defining them gives us mastery over them. When you take the time to articulate these thoughts and feelings, to write them down as best you can, you gain power over them. For identifying your problem loops, METAL is a useful model.

MIND GAME

——————

Name That Loop

For the rest of the day, try to "catch" your negative mind loops as they happen. Watch for signs of mental "pain" or friction, which are a good indicator of thought processes that need debugging.

Debug each negative thought loop down to its root problem using one of the three techniques:

- The Five Whys: Ask "Why?" five times.
- Worst-Case Scenario: What's the worst thing that could happen?
- Third-Person Perspective: What would you say if you were hearing this from someone else?

At the end of the day, write down each of the "root problems" you uncovered on your practice sheet, preferably using the METAL method.

In Part 1 of *Mind Hacking*, we've seen how the mind is a naturally noisy place and how we can cultivate focus and awareness of the mind's programming through regular concentration practice. Using the laser-like clarity that we develop through this practice, we can examine areas of our thinking where we have pain or difficulty, debugging our negative loops with skill and precision. This sets the stage for active reprogramming of the mind, which we'll cover next, in Part 2.

This is where things get fun.

PART TWO

IMAGINING

<IT'S ALL IN YOUR MIND>

"Imagination is more important than knowledge."
—Albert Einstein, as quoted on every dorm
room wall at every college ever

Albert Einstein may have been a genius, but he probably wasn't the best patent clerk.

Years before Steve Wozniak started building the world's largest computer company on his lunch breaks, another legendary figure was scribbling out equations at *his* day job. Einstein was a lowly government worker who toiled away at the Swiss patent office, reviewing patent applications. He had recently graduated from the Swiss Federal Institute of Technology with barely average grades, and no one would hire him as a physics teacher.[1]

One of Einstein's high school teachers, frustrated by his lack of obedience, had proclaimed that "nothing will ever become of you," and it looked as if he might be right. Day after day, Einstein was stuck in his low-level government job, a third-class patent clerk with little hope of escape. When he applied for a promotion to second-class patent clerk, he was turned down because his supervisor thought he didn't know enough about mechanical engineering!

What the job gave Einstein, however, was plenty of time to think. Whenever an idea would strike him, he would scribble down notes and tuck them into a drawer in his desk. (He jokingly called this drawer his "department of theoretical physics.") Einstein's revolutionary theories, and his most famous work, were achieved not by working in a lab or by performing physical experiments. They were developed *in his mind*.

Free from the typical constraints of academia, Einstein developed his theories as "thought experiments." For example: *What would you experience if you were in an elevator that went into freefall?* Or: *What would you see if you were riding a beam of light?* These were ideas that could not be easily tested, but reflecting upon them led Einstein to his world-changing ideas. First he did it in his head, *then* he did the math. There was one way to escape his day job, and that was *in his imagination*.

In a similar way, *your life* is a thought experiment. We've seen that your mind is constantly feeding you a stream of thoughts, most of which you accept without question. We can burn a lot of CPU cycles on these thoughts, which our mind spins into elaborate stories, some of which are downright crazy.

Jim arrives at work to learn that his company has been bought out by a larger competitor. He convinces himself that the new owners will downsize his job, and begins obsessively worrying over who will hire him after he's laid off. His mind begins spinning stories that he will never find a job in program management and he will end up managing an Arby's. (The truth is that Jim actually gets rolled into a better team at the new company.)

Lucy gets unfriended by her longtime college pal on social media. She spends the next few weeks heartbroken, wondering what she did to offend her and how they could have grown so distant. She convinces herself that she is not friendable, that no one wants to be close to her.

(The truth is that her college friend was trying to move her contacts over to a new account.)

Chris notices a small rash on his forearm. He ignores it at first, but when it grows larger, so do his anxieties. He researches "arm rash" on the Internet, finding the worst possible diseases, complete with lurid photos. He phones his doctor in a panic, convinced he is the first victim in a new pandemic of the Black Death. (The truth is, it's poison ivy.)

You probably have your own version of these ideas, which would be funny if they weren't so frightening. As you become more aware of your mind by practicing the exercises in the previous section, you get better at recognizing them for what they are: *imaginative works of fiction.*

But even though these stories start off in our imagination, they affect our actual lives. Jim spends hours working on new projects, trying to keep from getting fired. Lucy stops talking to her college friend, convinced they've had a falling-out. Chris is nearly in a panic by the time he sees the doctor. What's *true* is that each person experienced an initial event (a corporate buyout, an unfriending, a rash), but what's *false* is the imagined story that became an Oscar-nominated screenplay.

Every time you imagine how much your job sucks, or how you're still stuck in a loveless marriage, or how you'll never get in shape, you are repeating your loops. Over time, these loops become deeply held beliefs, influencing your day-in, day-out decisions that over the long haul determine the direction of your life. Ultimately your loops become self-fulfilling prophecies: if you think, *I'm no good at running*, you won't run; therefore, you'll be no good at running.

That's the bad news about imagination: if we don't know any better, it will carry us away. The good news is that *imagination, properly wielded, can also be used to come up with powerful new stories.*

You can choose what to imagine!

Our natural inclination is to think in terms of what we *do not* want: *I need to get out of this relationship*, or *It sucks to drive around in this beat-up car*, or

I don't want to sit in the cubicle next to the guy who farts. To rebuild our mind, and rebuild our lives, we have to be able to picture clearly *what it is we want.*

Pull yourself back from the mind movie for a moment and think about how you could rewrite those negative loops. You could just as easily imagine, *I can find a satisfying job,* or *I can work on this marriage,* or *I'm slapping on some spandex and going for a jog.* In your imagination, you can instantly create and destroy these ideas, like variables in code.

If you believe in those negative loops—if you think they're the way things have to be—I want to chip away at that belief. I've got my chisel and I am cracking away at the mortar that holds together the bricks that bind you. Eventually, I hope to open a hole in this wall and let a shaft of brilliant sunlight come streaming in.

I want to convince you that **imagination is real**. In some ways, it is more real than the world around you. And with a little training and practice, you can develop your power of imagination to not only change your life but to change the world around you.

Your world can become anything you can imagine.

Welcome to the Matrix

The man wears sunglasses and a trench coat. He sits across from a young computer programmer in a room with walls the sickly color of split-pea soup.

"The Matrix is everywhere," the man intones. "It is all around us. Even now, in this very room." Thunder crackles in the distance. "*It is the world that has been pulled over your eyes to blind you from the truth.*"

"What truth?" asks Neo, the bewildered computer geek.

Morpheus leans in. "That you are a slave," he responds. "Like everyone else, you were born into bondage. Born into a prison you cannot smell or taste or touch. A prison. *For your mind.*"

He produces a small silver case, then holds out two pills: one red, one blue.

"You take the blue pill, the story ends, you wake up in your bed and believe whatever you want to. You take the red pill, you stay in Wonderland, and I show you how deep the rabbit hole goes."

Neo hesitates, then reaches for the red pill. Morpheus warns him, "Remember, all I'm offering is the truth. Nothing more."

The scene that follows next in *The Matrix* is incredibly weird and difficult to explain, so we'll just say Neo experiences firsthand that he has indeed been living in a simulated reality, a "mind movie." As this artificial reality disintegrates, Neo comes to understand that the Matrix—this world he lived in—is nothing but computer code. *It can be reprogrammed.*

Neo joins a group of rebels who have learned to hack the Matrix, reentering the artificial reality they used to call home in order to free other enslaved humans by showing them the truth. And because they now know how the Matrix works, they can bend the physical laws of reality and give themselves superhuman powers, like the ability to dodge bullets while wearing floor-length trench coats. (For most people, trench coats are quite constricting.)

Like Neo, we, too, are in a kind of "prison of the mind." Our mental loops keep us trapped in this prison with invisible walls, convinced that our current reality is the *only* reality. But like *The Matrix* we can hack back into our minds, rewriting our mental code. Once again the key question is: *What do you want?*

Before I got sober, for example, I would feel incredibly awkward in face-to-face conversations, because I imagined that *I was no good with people.* I would be talking with someone, and all I could think about was how they were perceiving me. Was I standing up straight? Was I funny enough? Did I have a piece of kale in my teeth? It's difficult to be really engaged in a conversation when your mind is obsessing over your every potential flaw. This is why many of us drink: to get rid of that sense of awkward self-consciousness.

What did I want? I wanted to feel comfortable around people. After sobriety, one of my mind hacks was to start telling myself, *I'm good with people.* Through hundreds and thousands of repetitions of that simple idea, I was slowly able to turn things around, so that now I really *am* pretty good with people. It happens slowly, a gradual metamorphosis, but you *can* work on those old thoughts of why you suck and reimagine them as thoughts of positivity and self-esteem.

Let's take My Emotion-Thought-Action Loop from the previous section and start to imagine what shiny new METAL might look like.

Emotion	Thought(s)	Action(s)	New Loop
Anxiety about a new assignment at work	*I don't know if I can deliver this in a way that will make my boss happy.*	Doubting the results of my work, redoing the project multiple times, unnecessary overtime and stress	*I'm very good at this job.*
Depression about my relationship with my partner	*We're not as close as we were before, and we're drifting further apart.*	Getting angry at my partner over minor issues, passive-aggressive behavior, and frequent criticisms	*We are growing closer every day.*
Self-criticism over that stupid thing I said	*Why did I say that? Why did I say that? WHY DID I SAY THAT?*	Being self-conscious about everything I say to this person in the future	*I'm confident in everything I do and say.*
Regret about that decision I made in the past	*I shouldn't have done that. I wish I could go do it all over. My life would look so much better.*	Self-doubt and procrastination about making any decisions in the present	*I'm grateful that I am older and wiser, and making great decisions because of it.*
Worry about my career after graduation	*The job market is terrible. I have no experience. There are lots of other people more qualified than me.*	Reading gossip sites and watching funny llama videos instead of looking for a job	*I'm good enough, I'm smart enough, and doggone it, people like me.*

By developing the skill of imagination, you can learn to picture *what you want*, not just what you *don't* want. Just as a technology hacker finds a new use for an existing gadget (turning a leaf blower into a homemade hovercraft), you can construct new ways of thinking about yourself and the world. By choosing to think in larger, more positive terms, you begin to rewrite your personal reality in a larger, more positive direction. Your life gets not unimaginably better but *imaginably* better.

Now, imagine that Morpheus is standing beside you, offering *you* the choice between two pills. Which will you take?

Homemade Plato

I liked *The Matrix* better the first time, when it was called *The Allegory of the Cave*. It was a screenplay written by the ancient Greek dude Plato, and because the original story was a little confusing, I'll simplify it for modern times.

In *The Cave*, there are a bunch of prisoners chained to seats inside a movie theater. They're forced to watch the world's most boring movie: just the projector shining white light on the screen. Their heads are locked forward, like in *A Clockwork Orange*, which is a movie they never see. In fact, they never see *any* movie, just light and the occasional shadow.

This is because the prison warden is also the projectionist, and he paces around in the projection booth, frequently walking in front of the projector as he shouts at them. Sometimes his girlfriend comes over and they argue or have sex, so all the prisoners see is shadows and light, and all they hear is the distant sound of bickering or moaning.

After a few years of this, the prisoners begin to think that the shadows *are* the prison warden, or his girlfriend, or the other people that stop by.

"But how do the prisoners eat?" you might ask. "How do they go to the bathroom? Wouldn't they figure it out?" Plato's screenplay had a lot of plot holes, I'll admit. That's probably why it was in turnaround for thousands of years. But it gets better.

One day, one of the prisoners breaks free. Our protagonist sees the projectionist and his mind is blown. He walks out the doors of the theater and into the lobby. Popcorn! Candy! Starbucks! He walks outside, into the mall.

His eyes are dazzled by the overhead fluorescent lights. He can't make sense of any of it. It's so utterly different from his light/shadow reality that he struggles to come to grips with this "reality behind the reality."

Eventually, he goes back into the movie theater and tries to tell the other prisoners what's out there. "There's this crunchy yellow stuff you can eat, called *popcorn!*" he raves. "And this hot brown liquid called *coffee!* You buy it all with money, which is *valuable green paper!*"

The prisoners look at each other and begin to whisper, "Clearly, he's gone insane. Let this be a lesson to all of us: Whatever happens, *do not leave your seat.*"

The premise behind Plato's *Cave* (I don't think he ever wrote *Cave II: The Redemption*) was that most of us take physical reality at face value, but underneath, there is another world, a world of *ideas*. The ideas, in fact, are the *true* reality—they are, in a sense, more real than what we call "reality."

Think of how much of your personal reality starts in your imagination. You want to spend a night out with friends, you plan it out in your head first. If you desire to build a company, first you build it in your mind. Before you produce meaningfully, you produce it first mentally. *Your mind is the workshop for your life.*

The British physicist Sir Arthur Stanley Eddington was the Neil deGrasse Tyson of his day: an immensely popular science writer who became a household name during the 1920s and 1930s due to his clear, humorous explanations of difficult scientific topics. He liked to describe the universe not as a purely physical reality but as something more like a "great idea."

> It is difficult for the matter-of-fact physicist to accept the view that the substratum of everything is of mental character. But no one can deny that mind is the first and most direct thing in our experience, and all else is remote inference.[2]

It is *still* difficult to accept the view that "everything is of mental character." But once you accept that your mind is where your life starts, everything gets so much simpler. To change your life, change your mind. And *once* you change your mind, you can change your life in any way you can imagine.

Thinking of your world as a "great idea" really is a great idea.

The Reality Distortion Field

"Illusion is first of all needed to find the powers of which the self is capable."

—Paul Horgan, Pulitzer Prize–winning author

In February 1981, Bud Tribble, one of the key software developers on the original Macintosh computer, welcomed one of Apple's new employees, Andy Hertzfeld, by telling him they were scheduled to ship the Macintosh software in just ten months.

"Ten months?" Hertzfeld remarked. "That's impossible."

Tribble agreed. "The best way to describe the situation is a term from *Star Trek*," he explained. "*Steve Jobs has a reality distortion field.*"

It would make sense that a guy named Tribble would use a *Star Trek* reference. He was referring to a two-part episode entitled "The Menagerie," in which the crew finds a planet called Talos, whose inhabitants are able to create virtual realities in the minds of other people—or, as Tribble later put it, creating "their own new world through sheer mental force."

Tribble went on to explain this "reality distortion field" to his new employee: "In [Jobs's] presence, reality is malleable. He can convince anyone of practically anything. It wears off when he's not around, but it makes it hard to have realistic schedules."

Note that this was a veteran developer making this claim, not some woo-woo weirdo. Hertzfeld thought that Tribble was exaggerating—until he saw it for himself. Hertzfeld later wrote:

The reality distortion field was a confounding melange of a charismatic rhetorical style, an indomitable will, and an eagerness to bend any fact to fit the purpose at hand. Amazingly, the reality distortion field seemed to be effective even if you were acutely aware of it, although the effects would fade after Steve departed. We would often discuss potential techniques for grounding it . . . but after a while most of us gave up, accepting it as a force of nature.[3]

Jobs's "reality distortion field" was a personal refusal to accept limitations that stood in the way of his ideas, to convince himself that any difficulty was surmountable. This "field" was so strong that he was able to convince others that they, too, could achieve the impossible. It was an *internal* reality so powerful it also became an *external* reality. Whatever you may say about Jobs, he was a master mind hacker.

To use Tribble's phrase, Jobs created his "own new world through sheer mental force." Now, compare that with our typical approach: when confronted with a new idea, we quickly assess whether it seems feasible for us. *I'm terrible at talking to people*, we fret to ourselves at a club, and sit in the corner. Or: *I could invest my money in that stock, but knowing my luck, I'll probably lose it all.*

We might tell ourselves, *I'm a lousy runner*, or *I'm no good at math*. We might say, "Everyone in my family got divorced, so I will, too," or "I come from a long line of engineers, so that's why I don't do well with emotions." Think back to the problem loops you identified in the previous section. Most likely, these are *limitations* you've placed on yourself, or others, or the world—limitations that exist largely *in your mind*.

You have within yourself your own reality distortion field. What you consider "possible" and "impossible" for yourself are just ideas. They're loops that can be reprogrammed. You can find the boundaries of what you consider possible and consciously widen them. You can achieve the "impossible" by *training your mind to believe otherwise*.

Thinking "anything is possible" does not mean it's possible next week or even next year. We need to make a plan for what we can achieve, and do the work to make it a reality. (We'll cover this in Part 3.) But an attitude of "anything is possible" is the foundation from which we should begin. As the great author and naturalist John Muir proclaimed, "The power of imagination makes us infinite."

This is so much bigger than just reprogramming your negative thought loops. If you were learning to program and all you did was debug other people's code, you'd lose interest pretty quickly. But being able to build something *completely new and amazing* is the joy of hacking, and mind hacking is no different. As Mark Zuckerberg said about programming, "If you can code, you have the power to sit down and make something and no one can stop you." [4] Your life—your *future*—is a wide-open vista.

Consciously reshape your thoughts, and you can actively reshape the world around you. Once you think about it, anything is possible.

The Infinite Loop

"Space is big. Really big. You just won't believe how vastly, hugely, mind bogglingly big it is. I mean, you may think it's a long way down the road to the drugstore, but that's just peanuts to space." [5]

So begins the famous interplanetary travel guide *The Hitchhiker's Guide to the Galaxy*, preparing the adventurous traveler for the nearly unlimited variety of experiences available while hitchhiking around space. From the breathtaking beaches of B'bbahl (where time flows backward, so it is possible to leave your two-week vacation earlier than you arrived) to the Nightclub at the Beginning of the Universe (where you can watch the Big Bang unfold beneath a pulsing disco beat), anything is possible in space.

Similarly, your mind is a vast unexplored landscape—we might even say *infinite*, since there is no limit to what can be imagined. It is a universe of possibilities, a limitless horizon of potential. *Our minds have unlimited imagining power.* This is not just some phrase to put on an inspirational poster underneath a photo of a man hanging on to the talons of an eagle in flight. It's a simple and obvious fact. *Your mind is as big as you can imagine it to be.*

Dr. Ellen Langer, the longest-running professor of psychology at Harvard, came up with an ingenious experiment to test the effects of imagination on aging. She first created an environment straight out of the 1950s, down to the smallest details: a black-and-white TV playing *Ed Sullivan* clips, an old-fashioned radio playing Perry Como. Then she recruited eight men in their seventies to live in this environment for five days.

When they entered this virtual reality, Langer asked the seniors not just to reminisce about their younger years but to make a psychological attempt to *be* the person they were in 1959. In other words, to *imagine they were young again.* "We have good reason to believe that if you are successful at this," she told them, "you will feel as you did in 1959."[6]

Throughout the experiment, as the senior citizens talked about current events (events of the 1950s), they were encouraged to talk about them in the present tense. There were no mirrors, no current photographs, nothing that would spoil the illusion of being young again.

The results were astounding. At the end of their stay, the elderly subjects were tested on a number of age-related factors, from memory to dexterity, and were shown to significantly improve versus a control group. A panel of independent judges said they sat up straighter and looked younger. Although it seems impossible, *even their sight got better.* As the *New York Times Magazine* reported, they "had put their minds in an earlier time, and their bodies went along for the ride."

Our minds are as large as we imagine them to be. We instinctively know this when we refer to a "small-minded person" as someone who is petty or bigoted, and "an exceptionally large mind" to talk about someone like Stephen Hawking. Indeed, Hawking is a terrific example of someone who did not allow his physical handicap to limit his greatness. How many of us, if confined to a wheelchair with nothing but a few eye movements to communicate, would approach the world-changing creative output of Hawking?

I've been lucky enough to work with a number of entrepreneurial advisors. What the best advisors do is continually expand your sense of what's possible: they take your initial number, then add a zero. If you want to grow a $20 million business, they encourage you to think about a $200 million business. I've found this a useful concept as we've grown Media Shower, our content marketing company: *Keep adding a zero.* Always think about the next level of scale: from 100 to 1,000 customers, from 1,000 to 10,000 customers, from 10,000 to 100,000 customers, and so on.

After I got sober and began identifying my problem loops, I started to think about how I was going to reprogram those loops. As I realized my reprogramming could become as big as I imagined, it became an intellectual challenge for me to think up the biggest loops I could. While I suppose an infinite loop would technically be the largest, I found the idea of an *exponentially increasing loop* to be more exciting. Now, each night before I go to sleep, I reprogram my mind with this loop:

```
> My ability to bring amazing things into the world is
  exponentially increasing.
```

What will this simple thought bring over a lifetime of repeating it? I intend to find out.

You can believe that your mind creates your internal reality, and to a large degree your external reality as well. Using imagination, you can learn to not only be happier and think more positively but to create bigger and better things for yourself and the world: to create your own "reality distortion field."

Thinking big, however, is easier said than done! Developing big plans requires programming **your best possible future**, a pleasurable technique of mind hacking that you'll learn next.

<YOUR BEST POSSIBLE FUTURE>

"If you can't conceive of things that don't exist, you can't create anything new. If you can't dream up worlds that might be, then you are limited to the worlds other people describe."

—Robert S. Root-Bernstein and
Michele M. Root-Bernstein, *Sparks of Genius*[1]

What do you want?

Perhaps you have relatively modest dreams, like graduating with honors, or finding your soul mate, or becoming a millionaire. Maybe your ambitions are greater, like eradicating a major disease, or building a world-changing charity, or running a nation. Or perhaps we're *really* thinking big together: inventing a new branch of science, or colonizing other planets, or improving the mental state of the human race.

It's easy to figure out what you *don't* want: they're the things you're always complaining about, to yourself and everyone else. But do you know what you *want*? Have you written it down? If you get the dreaded job interview question "Where do you see yourself in twenty years?" will you have a thoughtful answer, or will you draw a blank?

In a fascinating study by psychologist Laura King,[2] college students were asked to write for twenty minutes a day about their "best possible future self." She challenged them to stretch their imaginations to envision the *biggest, best-case scenario* for their lives. After just a few days, the test subjects who spent the time imagining a positive future were significantly *happier* and *more positive* than a control group. Another longer-term study by King showed that writing positively made them *healthier* as well, with fewer visits to doctors.[3]

Here's a mini-version of King's experiment: Close your eyes and imagine your life in ten years, with your best possible outcome. Try to picture your best possible future in vivid detail. Where will you live? What will you do for work? For fun? Will you have a partner? What kinds of friends will you have? How much money will you have? What will your mind look like?

Go on. Close your eyes and see what you find. I'll wait.

Loading

Most people have a vague idea of what they want out of life, but they've never taken the time to imagine it. If you ask them point-blank, they might give you a vague answer like "More money," or "Happiness," or "A pony."

Instead of captaining their own ship, most people float wherever the waves take them. How is it that something as important as our *future*, the thing that should matter above all else, gets so little attention? I believe the answer is simple: *imagination is difficult.*

When I try to imagine the exercise above, it's like seeing a series of images flashing through my mind, but dark and hazy, like a grainy video. If I feed more questions into the stream, I get more pictures. For example: *In my best possible future, how do I want to feel? Who are my celebrity friends? How many zebras do I own? Have I learned to levitate?* Each one of these brings a series of accompanying images, slippery and fluid. It's hard to hold on to any of them, as they're instantly replaced with something else.

Worse, my mind keeps wanting to change the subject, to follow some other train of thought—the disobedient dog again. So keeping it focused on the object of my imagination, *to persist without giving up*, is quite difficult.

I challenge you to spend the next five minutes really picturing what you want your life to look like in ten years. If you can't invest five minutes thinking about what you want to become, you have to seriously question your priorities. These five minutes could mean the difference between a life of confusion and sorrow and a life of happiness and fulfillment. What could be more important than that?

In fact, unless you live your life under the assumption that riches, relationships, and rock stars are going to suddenly fall from the sky, it's just an obvious fact that you're going to need to figure out what you want from life. And the way you figure that out is in your mind. *You imagine it.*

Take five minutes and imagine. I'm patient.

Loading

Does your experience agree with mine? Did you find it incredibly challenging to spend five minutes in imagination? It's odd that something as important as your personal future—arguably *the most important thing in your life*—would be so difficult to focus on. But that's the way it is with imagination.

Imagination is hard mental work. To really imagine well, in my experience, is as difficult as actual *physical* work. Note: I am not talking about following the "mind movie" or being caught in a daydream; I'm talking about actively imagining, focusing your mind on creating a clear mental picture. It *feels* more like work. It feels like moving things around with your mind, creating mental schemas or blueprints or plans.

In mind hacking, we learn to identify the "feel" of imagining, and not to shy away from it but to actively engage in it, with persistence and playfulness. It should feel like **manipulating mental objects**: real manual work, moving things around. Imagine digging, or sculpting, with your mind. Only through exercising this active visualizing component (like a muscle) can we build up its power and strength.

One Click, One Idea

In 1997, Amazon founder Jeff Bezos was having lunch with Amazon's first employee, Shel Kaphan, and his programmer Peri Hartman. Websites at the time were still clunky, and Bezos was obsessed then, as he is now, with making it as easy as possible for customers to order products from Amazon.com. He issued them a crazy challenge: *Invent a way for customers to order from Amazon with a single click.*[4]

The idea of "1-Click Ordering" is now so natural that we barely notice it. Back then, the idea was nuts. This was a time when the idea of *ordering products from a website* still made many people nervous. *Will my credit card be stolen? How can I see the products first? What if I need to return it?* Ordering online seemed risky and weird, much less ordering with *one click.*

The development team worked like mad to develop the single-click or-dering feature. When they showed the first prototype of 1-Click to Bezos, it ended up requiring *twelve clicks*. They explained to Bezos there were certain steps you simply couldn't eliminate: a customer had to give Amazon a mailing address, for example, and a credit card number. Customers needed a confir-mation screen so they wouldn't place an order by accident.

"One click," Bezos replied.

After many more hours of deliberation, the team came back to Bezos with an improved prototype. This one allowed customers to *save* their mailing ad-dress and credit card information in their accounts (another crazy idea for the time), then make a purchase with one click. But they still needed one more click to confirm that the customer wanted to make the purchase.

There was still just one problem: their one-click ordering system required *two clicks*.

"One click," Bezos demanded.

Finally, the team hit upon the solution: let customers place the order with one click, and if they placed it by accident, let them easily cancel the purchase. It seems obvious in retrospect, but good ideas always do. As soon as Amazon showed it was possible, other online retailers rushed to copy the idea. The idea that had recently seemed impossible now seemed indispensable to online success.

And in fact it was. Thanks to the power of that idea, and many others like it, Amazon grew to dominate the online retail industry. And it all started in Bezos's frighteningly large imagination.

We have a strange attitude toward imagination. When we see it in geniuses like Jeff Bezos, we call it "vision." When we see it in children, we call it "cute." When we see it in ourselves, we often call it "a dumb idea" or "a crazy thought." In reality, however, it's the same skill: the skill of *developing a clear mental picture*.

Bezos used nothing but his imagination to transform reality. What did he actually *do*? His developers did all the work. Trust me that Bezos was not mocking up wireframes and writing functions. All he did was create a clear mental picture in his mind of what he wanted, then ride the development team until they got it done.

Let's picture the world of ideas, the world of imagination, as being something like the working memory of a computer. This is a state where the computer is holding a great deal of data "in its head." It hasn't been written to a hard drive or saved to the cloud—if you pull the plug, you lose it all. It's a kind of mental workspace.

Our minds provide that same mental workspace, a place where we can dream, develop, and refine the ideas that will eventually shape our physical world. Imagination is not just a toy for children; it's the blueprint for reality. And in fact we use imagination every day: to decide where to meet our friends for dinner, or how to tackle a difficult algorithm. It happens up here before it happens out there.

How is it that we do not teach this in schools? There are no high school Imagination teams, no standardized tests for Imagining, no extra credit given for drawing a picture of an insane motorized animal on your biology homework. You do not get an A in history class for writing a short story where Eleanor Roosevelt fights Nazis by shooting lasers from her nipples.

Perhaps this is why we do not value imagination for its fundamental importance: as a mental workspace where everything begins. **Imagination has reality.** It is real in the same way that a blueprint is real to the finished building. It is real in the same way that a schema is real to the database. It is real in the same way that an idea jotted down on a whiteboard is real to the business itself.

Put another way, imagination is a *representation that precedes the thing itself.* And you—the "you" that is separate from "your mind"—are able to summon it at will. It is an awesome power.

Imagination,
then realization.

In 1962, legendary science fiction writer and geek hero Arthur C. Clarke wrote an essay entitled "Hazards of Prophecy: The Failure of Imagination." In that essay, he famously declared that "any sufficiently advanced technology is indistinguishable from magic." As an example, if we took a human from the Dark Ages and showed him a modern computer or microwave oven, he would be convinced they were powered by sorcery and witchcraft.

Looked at from Clarke's perspective, our imagination is both *an incredibly advanced technology*, and *indistinguishable from magic.* The fact that you can conjure up entire worlds in your mind—that you can visualize the future course of reality—really *is* like a kind of magic.

However, we must be careful to avoid falling into "magical thinking." I am regularly amazed at how many well-educated people suffer from one of the two following superstitions:

- **Magical negative thinking:** the belief that if we think or say something terrible, it will instantly come to pass. You can spot this thinking through the use of phrases like "God forbid" or "knock on wood," or putting a little too much faith in fortune cookies. Certainly we are constantly imagining things that do *not* come to pass; we do not need to be afraid of our own dark thoughts.

- **Magical positive thinking:** the belief that all we need to do is think positive thoughts, then sit back and relax as life "manifests" them for us. When I talk about imagination being like a kind of magic, I am not saying that imagination will make things magically appear. That requires hard work, and the techniques you'll learn in Part 3. But, consistently applied and mixed with work, it will make things *more likely* to appear, just as 1-Click eventually appeared for Jeff Bezos.

It is a simple and obvious fact that nothing of value can be achieved until you first see it in your mind. So tell me: When you unlock that secret treasure chest in your mind, what do you see?

Feel, Do, Have, Give, and Be [5]

Now that you're warmed up, we'll play five easy imagination games. The goal is to simply write down *one* result for each of the following mind games.

The Mood Chip. A group of biotech-hardware entrepreneurs have developed a revolutionary new "mood chip" that can be surgically implanted into your brain. Originally developed to treat Alzheimer's, they've found that it can treat a wide array of symptoms, from depression to ADD. The chip can be programmed to give you a "feeling boost" in any emotional direction you like; in fact, different versions of the chip are marketed with names like Happy, Calm, Focused, Inquisitive, Ambitious, Compassionate, Decisive, Empowered, and Positive. (Think of these in relation to the problem loops you identified earlier.)

You have the funds to buy exactly one Mood Chip. Close your eyes and imagine: *What is the one word that describes how you would like to feel?*

The $50 Million Inheritance. It's a story straight out of a movie. A great-great-great-aunt whom you've never met passes away, leaving behind a small fortune. Her will stipulates that her estate must stay within the family; because she was quite old herself, all her relatives are now deceased, except for you. She lived very frugally, so other than selling her mobile home and twelve cases of Diet Pepsi, the rest of her $50 million fortune is yours, right now, in cash. You now have the freedom to do anything you want in life, from building your own monster truck to climbing K2.

Close your eyes and imagine: *What is the one thing you've always wanted to do?*

The Genie in the Lamp. Some people buy scratch tickets; you buy antique lamps. You travel the world, shopping in obscure Middle Eastern bazaars, in hopes that you will finally find the enchanted lamp that contains a wondrous genie. One day you return to your hotel, shopping bags full of lamps, and find that you've hit the jackpot: not one but *two* lamps contain a genie, each granting you one wish. Knowing the genii are crafty and will do anything to trick you out of your wish, you pull a meta-wish and wish the first genie to force the second genie to honor his word. Now you have one wish left.

Close your eyes and imagine: *What is the one thing you would like to have?*

Your Evolution Contribution. The legendary hedge fund manager Ray Dalio, in his excellent book *Principles*, talks of evolution from a very practical viewpoint. He describes evolution as the desire to "get better," stating, "society rewards those who give it what it wants."[6] In other words, the way to get rich or be "successful" in worldly terms is not to chase money or success but to *contribute something genuinely* *useful to the world.* This is ideally something you're passionate about, whether raising great children, writing great music, or developing a great new compression algorithm.

Close your eyes and imagine: *What is the one thing you would like to contribute to the world?*

The Funeral Speech. One day, both you and I will be dead. (Sorry to break the news.) During our funerals (I don't know how we both have funerals on the same day, I'm just trying to make you feel better about being dead), our loved ones will stand up and say a few words about our lives, nicely condensed into a ten-minute speech, because a lot of people will be anxious to get to the sandwich trays at the reception. When they give your eulogy, what is it you want them to say about you? In other words, *who do you want to be?*

Close your eyes and imagine: *What is the one adjective that describes who you would like to be?*

MIND GAME

The Five Words

Complete the five imagination games in this section. Write down one word for each. (It's better to get it done than get it perfect. You can always add more later.)

Write down the five words on your practice sheet.

<CREATING POSITIVE THOUGHT LOOPS>

B enjamin Franklin was a geek.

"Throughout his life," Walter Isaacson notes in his excellent biography *Benjamin Franklin: An American Life*, "he loved immersing himself in minutiae and trivia in a manner so obsessive that today it might be described as geeky."[1] He points to Franklin's methodical research, unbounded curiosity, and constant inventiveness (note our Analyze, Imagine, and Reprogram framework again!) on topics as diverse as ballooning, education, electricity, eyeglasses, fire safety, heating technology, music, politics, and weather.

Franklin was also a master mind hacker. Hundreds of years before people were using fitness-tracking devices, he came up with a self-improvement experiment that let him track his mind hacking progress in a measurable, scientific way. As described in his autobiography, Franklin gave his experiment the lofty title of the "Moral Perfection Project." He began by laying out a set of thirteen virtues that he wished to develop in himself:[2]

- **Temperance:** moderating eating and drinking

- **Silence:** speaking only when it benefits others or yourself

- **Order:** letting everything have its place

- **Resolution:** resolving to do what you should; doing without fail what you resolve

- **Frugality:** being careful with money and resources; wasting nothing

- **Industry:** working hard but efficiently

- **Sincerity:** meaning what you say; saying what you mean

- **Justice:** wronging no one, either by what you do or don't do

- **Moderation:** avoiding extremes and letting go of grudges

- **Cleanliness:** keeping your body, clothes, home, and workspace clean

- **Tranquility:** calmly accepting small misfortunes that are common and unavoidable

- **Chastity:** moderating sexual activity

- **Humility:** imitating "Jesus and Socrates"

These virtues became Franklin's *positive thought loops*. His method of re-programming his mind with these values was both simple and ingenious. In a diary, he made a simple grid with columns representing each day of the week, and rows representing each of the thirteen virtues:

	S	M	T	W	T	F	S
T							
S	••	•		•		•	
O	•	•	•		•	•	•
R			•		•		
F		•			•		
I			•				
S							
J							
M							
Cl.							
T							
Ch							
H							

Reasoning that it would be easier to tackle one virtue at a time, he listed them in order of importance, so that one habit built upon the next. Temperance came first, because you couldn't make progress on the other virtues if you were drunk all the time. Once you had Temperance under control, it would be easier to tackle Silence. Once Silence was conquered, Order would follow, and so on.

Each day, Franklin reviewed his progress across all thirteen virtues, marking with a black spot any day in which he did not live up to his ideal. But each week he also had a "target virtue" (or thought loop) that he would strive to keep clear for the entire week. Thus, in the first week, his thought loop would be focused on Temperance. Having strengthened that virtue, he would focus on Silence in the second week, and so on.

Since there are fifty-two weeks in a year, Franklin was able to go through the list of thirteen virtues precisely four times in a year—a mathematical system any geek can appreciate. Perhaps Franklin expected to be done with it in a year, but he ended up using the system for most of his life. "I was surprised to find myself so much fuller of faults than I had imagined," Franklin recalled later, "but I had the satisfaction of seeing them diminish."

Indeed, Franklin's life is powerful testimony that these positive thought loops worked: although he was only human, he died an accomplished and respected man who certainly left the world a better place. Not only did he invent the lightning rod, bifocals, odometer, urinary catheter, and swim fins, he also invented the self-help book.

Positive vs. Negative

Multiple studies show that we respond better to positive than negative feedback. One of my favorite examples is the "Speed Camera Lottery," an experiment run in Stockholm, Sweden. In many cities, speed cameras are used to automatically issue tickets when a motorist is caught driving over the speed limit. Kevin Richardson, a gaming producer for Nickelodeon, had an idea to flip the model on its head.

In his version of the speed camera, everyone who was caught driving *under* the speed limit would be entered into a lottery to *win* a portion of the speeding fines. In other words, drive *over* and you could get a ticket, drive *under* and you could win it.

Richardson's idea was tested out on a street in Stockholm. The results were fascinating. As the *New York Times* reported, "Average speed before the installation of the Speed Camera Lottery sign on a multilane street was 32 kilometers an hour. That figure dropped to 25 kilometers an hour during a three-day test, despite the device's inability to issue financial penalties."[3]

"Thinking of all the interesting ways we can penalize a few bad or distracted apples," Richardson was quoted, "is a mis-distribution of energy and attention." While this is true for distracted drivers, it's also true for our distracted minds. Once we become aware of our negative thought loops, we may start berating or penalizing ourselves for them. Just as with math, adding two negatives does not bring you to positive.

Still, negative feedback feels more "natural." When your child is climbing on top of the glass coffee table with a hammer, the most natural thing in the world is to scream, "NO!" My wife, who is an excellent parent of our two kids, taught me early on to resist the natural urge to say "No" and to instead *reframe it in the positive*. What is it that you *want* your kids to do? "Hammer in the garage," or "toy hammer only," or "shop eBay for new coffee table" are more constructive alternatives, because then the kids know what is *acceptable*.

Your mind is like a child. You need to condition it by continually reinforcing what you *want* it to do, not what you *don't* want it to do. If you think, *I don't want to feel anxious anymore*, or *I don't want to fail at work*, or *I don't want my life to look like this*, you're just defining the *absence* of the negative loop. It doesn't work to just cut out the problem code; *you have to rewrite it*.

It's more work to define what you want. It's harder to tell kids what they *should* be doing than to shout "No!" It's more difficult to explain to your partner or your family or your friends what you *need* than what's annoying you. But if you don't take the time to do it—if you can't articulate it to yourself and to someone else—then you're expecting the world to figure it out for you and serve it up like a robotic butler.

The Story of *The Story of Mel*

One of the classic pieces of hacker literature is a text document called *The Story of Mel*. Originally circulated on the Usenet newsgroup net.jokes, the story recounts the godlike programming abilities of a developer named Mel. Written in a reverent poetry-prose, the story has the cadence and feel of a piece of holy scripture.

Little is known about Mel, but subsequent generations of geeks have theorized he was an actual person: Mel Kaye, who wrote the software for the

1959 Royal McBee LGP-30 computer. Mel had created a blackjack game for the LGP-30, one of the first of its kind. The Royal McBee sales reps would take the LGP-30 to trade shows, where they would let prospective customers play the blackjack game. It's hard to remember there was a day when most people had never played a computer game, and the experience was so thrilling that it usually sold the LGP-30 on the spot, even though it was a business computer.

There was only one problem: Mel's blackjack game was *too* good. Sometimes the prospective customers *lost*, if you can imagine that. Concerned they were losing out on valuable sales opportunities, the Royal McBee sales reps approached Mel and told him the game was "too fair." They asked if he could modify the blackjack game so they could secretly flip a switch on the LGP-30 when they wanted to let prospective customers win.

Mel was morally opposed to this change. His code was statistically perfect, an elegant representation of real-world blackjack odds. How *dare* they ask him to insert an error into his perfect simulation! After getting some heat from above, Mel reluctantly complied. When he tested the "cheat switch," however, he found the computer cheated in the opposite direction, *so the computer always won*. He was delighted with this hack, of course, and eventually left the company without fixing it.

Enter the author of the story, a programmer named Ed Nather, who was brought into Royal McBee and asked to fix Mel's code. As he began digging into the masterpiece that Mel had left behind, he was astounded by the elegance and genius of Mel's code.

> *I have often felt that programming is an art form,*
> *whose real value can only be appreciated*
> *by another versed in the same arcane art;*
> *there are lovely gems and brilliant coups*
> *hidden from human view and admiration, sometimes forever,*
> *by the very nature of the process.*

You can learn a lot about an individual
just by reading through his code,
even in hexadecimal.
Mel was, I think, an unsung genius.[4]

Mel refused the help of any compilers or assemblers; he wrote in straight hex code, which looks like this:

```
> 79 6f 75 20 61 72 65 20 6e 6f 74 20 79 6f 75 72 20 6d 69 6e 64
```

The author writes reverently of Mel's machine-level hacks, such as "writing the innermost parts of his program loops first, so they would get first choice of the optimum address locations on the drum"—in other words, optimizing his code at the lowest possible level so that his programs would run with maximum efficiency on the LGP 30. Mel and the computer were one.

In the end, the author is so awestruck by Mel's coding mastery that he feels he cannot make any changes; it would be like touching up the *Mona Lisa*'s smile. He tells his boss he can't figure it out and writes this homage to Mel instead, in which Mel becomes the archetype of the "Real Programmer," the one to whom all other programmers aspire.

When we choose our positive thought loops, we are looking for that same sense of efficiency and optimization. When you think of the five goals you wrote in the previous chapter, what is the thought loop that will get you there? Choose your thought loops carefully, for they will determine the future direction of your life.

Constructing New Loops

The key to constructing positive thought loops is looking for *alternative* or *balanced* thoughts to replace the negative things that you've been telling yourself for years. Instead of automatically repeating the negative thoughts when certain situations arise, you want your mind to automatically repeat these positive thoughts instead. And as with Mel, you want to strive for *precision* and *elegance* in the wording of these loops.

For example, Jim's boss gives the team their monthly sales goals on the first of each month. Jim always has a nagging feeling of doom in the week leading up to it: *I'm not good enough, I won't meet my goals, I'll fail and be fired.* Instead, Jim could construct a positive thought loop like:

```
> I'm good at my job.
```

Or even better:

```
> I'm the top salesperson in my office.
```

Or better still:

```
> I'm brilliant at helping my company and our customers
  succeed.
```

Note with this last loop, he is enlarging his boundaries of what is possible, not just focusing on keeping his job by a thread, but actively adding value to the world.

Take Robbie, who is still feeling guilty over the fact that she argued with her father a week before he died. Whenever someone mentions death, or sometimes when she's just sitting at her desk, her mind flashes back to that moment and she thinks, *I'm a horrible daughter.* Her new positive loop could read:

```
> I'm a good daughter.
```

Or even better:

```
> I'm a good person.
```

Or better still:

```
> I'm at peace with myself, and getting better every day.
```

Note that the example of Jim is triggered by an external event, and the example of Robbie is triggered by an internal event. The negative thought loop that gets kicked off in each of them is similar: a feeling of *not being good enough*. As they become aware of these thought loops through the concentration games and identification techniques in the previous section, they are now armed with a powerful tool: *an alternative thought*.

Let's take a final example, which is very close to my heart (and lungs): getting free of alcohol and drugs. In the first few weeks of sobriety, there was only one thought going through my head: *I will never have fun again*. I was sure that lifelong sobriety was a ticket to boredom and unhappiness: no more drunken cow-tipping in Vermont, no more riding kiddie coasters while high as a hang glider. I suppose I could have thought:

```
> Sobriety is fun.
```

That felt like an outright lie. I could have thought:

```
> I'm happy to be sober.
```

I'm glad I settled on this positive loop:

```
> I'm grateful for my sobriety.
```

There is a great deal of research on the transformative power of thankfulness. In a series of studies by psychologists Robert A. Emmons and Michael E. McCullough,[5] three groups of people were given a different writing assignment for several weeks. One group listed five things for which they were grateful, one group listed five things that annoyed them, and a control group listed five things that had taken place during the week.

The results were dramatic: those in the "gratitude" group felt better about their lives, were physically healthier, slept better, spent more time exercising, were more likely to offer support to others, and were more optimistic about the future. A follow-up survey sent to the spouses and partners of participants confirmed that they noticed a positive difference as well.

The researchers struggled to define thankfulness, but the definition I like best is "savoring the positive circumstances of life." There are many positive circumstances in your life, whether that's your health, your friends, your intellectual capacity, your job, or just the fact that you're reading this book. On a daily basis, you can find *something* to appreciate, whether it's a good meal, a fine sunset, or a hearty laugh.

Feeding this gratefulness into your positive loops can have a powerful, life-altering impact, as it did for me. By repeating *I'm grateful for my sobriety*, day in and day out, I have found that I genuinely *am* grateful for my sobriety. I've gone from seeing it as a curse to a blessing—in fact, my sobriety is now like a precious treasure.

Choosing Your Loops

In the Academy Award–winning movie *Inception*, Leonardo DiCaprio leads a different kind of mind hacking team. *Inception* is a mind-bending science-fiction heist movie about a team that hacks not into bank vaults but into people's *minds* as they sleep. Using a secret military technology, DiCaprio's team is able to enter a "shared dream" with their target without that person's knowledge, even implanting an idea into the person's subconscious, a technique called "inception."

As the movie progresses, we learn the backstory: DiCaprio and his wife once entered a shared dream, where they spent fifty years together in this alternate world, building massive cityscapes and seemingly growing old together. His wife began to fall in love with the dream reality, never wishing to return to "real life." Unable to convince her, DiCaprio secretly placed an idea into her subconscious: *This is not real.*

The idea took root, and they finally woke up from their shared dream, to find that only three hours had passed. But that idea—*This is not real*—was so deeply planted in his wife's mind that she could not escape it, even when she was back in the "real world." Convinced she was *still* dreaming, she asked DiCaprio to jump off a building with her, before making the leap herself.

The movie contains three or four layers of meta-goodness, dreams within dreams within dreams, and leaves you with deep, unsettling questions about what reality really *is*. One of the critical messages of *Inception* is that implanting an idea in someone's mind can have a far-reaching impact on the person's life—for good as well as bad.

We want to use care in choosing our mental loops. If you're writing code to regulate an automatic braking system or land a plane, a bug can literally result in lost lives. Similarly, choosing a loop like *I'm the most important person in the world* or *I have absolute power over all my enemies*, repeated millions of times, can lead to behaviors that are ultimately destructive to you and the world. Put another way: Be careful what you wish for.

Remember, *your loops create your thoughts, your thoughts create your actions, and your actions create your life.* This is not meant to paralyze you with indecision (a surprisingly common problem among geeks) but to encourage you to consider your positive loops carefully. Here are some tips that may help:

- **Include the word "I."** Instead of *Self-confidence*, think: *I am self-confident.* Frame it in the first person, as if you are in control (which you are).

- **Ask:** *What do I want?* As with training a child or dog, keep it in the positive. Instead of *I'm not so self-critical*, try *I'm gentle with myself.*

- **Think big.** Think: *How can I enlarge my sense of what's possible?* Instead of *My business is making $20 million*, try *I'm a successful entrepreneur, adding massive value to the world.*

- **Create value.** Ask yourself how you can add maximum value not just to yourself but to society. Instead of *My wife and I get along* or *I have* *a successful marriage*, try something like *Our relationship is a model to the world*. Have fun with it!

Take the five goals from Section 2.2 and write a positive thought loop corresponding with each. These are meant to correspond with each of the following goals:

- **Feel.** From "The Mood Chip," how do you want to feel? Peaceful? Confident? Happy? Thinking back to your debugging techniques, look for the positive alternatives that you'd like to use to counteract your negative thoughts and feelings. Use these as your +2 Weapons of Mental Fortitude. For example, *I am strong, secure, and confident*; *I am mentally calm, poised, and relaxed*; or *I am comfortable in my own skin*.

- **Do.** From "The $50 Million Inheritance," what experience would you like to have in life? You may want to make a "moonshot goal," a big dream to pursue over your lifetime, or you may want to start with a shorter-term goal, something in the next year. For example, *I'm an accomplished traveler* or *I'm making the dean's list*.

- **Have.** From "The Genie in the Lamp," what thing would you like to own? I believe we can run into trouble by focusing too much on material possessions, but this one can be fun if we concentrate on how they can add value to society. For example, *I own a beautiful house, where we throw many fine parties*, or *I have my own jet, which I use to host my private mind hacking retreats*.

- **Give.** From "Your Evolution Contribution," what is it that you want to give back to the world? Remember that society generally rewards those who give it what it wants, in equal measure to the value created—so the bigger you think, the greater your potential reward. *I am eradicating malaria* and *I am making Internet access available to the entire planet* are great goals, but so is *I am creating music that benefits the world* and *I am raising a magnificent family*.

- **Be.** From "The Funeral Speech," who is it that you want to be? This is not what you want other people to *say* about you but what kind of person you want to *be*, at your core. Ben Franklin's list of thirteen virtues are an excellent place to start, as he consolidated them from many centuries of great philosophers and thinkers before him. For example, *I am trustworthy, always following through on my promises*, or *I am generous, freely giving of my talents to benefit the world.*

Choosing these loops can be hard work, and if you already suffer from the curse of perfectionism, you may just need to write *I give things my best effort and happily move on*, thus giving it your best effort and happily moving on.

As much as I've said about choosing your loops well, I now want to encourage you to actually *make a choice*. The award-winning psychologist M. Scott Peck once said that as long as our will is firmly committed toward the good, we can trust that our subconscious is at least one step ahead of our conscious and thus feel secure in our decisions.[6] Besides, just as with coding, you can always rewrite your positive loops later.

MIND GAME

Writing Your Positive Loops

Complete the five imagination games in this chapter. Write down each positive thought loop on the practice sheet at the end of the book. Focus on getting it done, not getting it perfect; you can always rewrite your code later.

You've now learned how to become aware of your mind, identify your negative thinking, and properly code positive thought loops to drive your mind in new directions of happiness and success. One thing still remains, however: *you have to do the work.*

If we leave off here, we are like the programmer who dreams up an amazing new app but never finishes it. We are like the aspiring musician who dreams of the stage but rarely practices. We are like the person with big dreams but who exerts little effort in bringing them to fruition.

In the next section, you'll learn techniques for *reprogramming* your mind. These are the day-in, day-out practices that you'll use to bring your ideas into the world. Backed by research and proven by science, these mind hacks will teach you how to make your dreams a reality.

Let the true mind hacking begin.

PART THREE

REPROGRAMMING

<WRITE>

Visiting the Thomas Edison National Historical Park in West Orange, New Jersey, should be on every geek's list of things to do in life.

Advertised as "Where Modern America Was Invented,"[1] It's an enormous brick building where, for more than forty years, Edison's team of geniuses turned out innovation after innovation, including the motion picture camera and movies, improved phonographs and sound recordings, and electric inventions like the alkaline storage battery. It was the Google of its day.

Edison is remembered today as a prolific inventor (over one thousand patents in his name), but perhaps his most important invention was *the process of invention itself.* The meta-invention of *how to make more inventions* is Edison's true legacy. Edison invented the modern research and development facility, and if you go to West Orange, you can still walk through it.

It's fascinating, and instructive, to see how Edison

laid out the complex. Tucked away in a corner of his expansive office was a small bed. Edison was a believer in the power of power naps: after ruminating on a difficult problem, he would retire in the corner for a microsleep, letting his mind work on a solution. When the idea came to him, he would hurry to his desk and **write it down**.

He would then rush upstairs to his second, more modest office, where he did his true "inventing." Here he would take the initial idea and sketch it out, making rough drawings of the idea that he wanted to pull into reality.

Next door to this office was a drafting room, where a team of draftsmen would take his ideas and begin drawing up formal plans. What parts would be needed? What materials would they be made of? Wrestling with these questions, with occasional input from the master, they would work up large-scale drawings from which the invention could now be built.

From there, the drawings went to a machine shop full of small electric tools. Frequently they needed to build machines *to build the machines* that would build the inventions. In this first shop, they could fabricate any small parts needed. These parts went below to a large-scale machine shop, a huge loft space filled with motorized pulleys, belts, and gears that could provide the power to manufacture the invention itself. Thomas Edison once bragged about his facility, "We can build anything from a lady's watch to a locomotive."[2]

From an idea, to paper, to plans, to machining, to manufacturing, to a finished product: it was an early prototype of today's R & D labs. I want to highlight what Edison did first when his mammoth mind presented him with an idea to feed into that amazing system. In order to turn that idea into a reality, *he wrote it down*.

There is a power and a magic in writing things down that we take for granted, because we do it so often. First, an idea is only in our mind, with no expression in the physical world. Then, with a few strokes of a pencil or a few awkward taps of our thumbs, that idea is now a *thing*. True, it may only be a *representation* of the thing, but it's still here, in this world.

Writing is a bridge, or a gateway, between the world of mind and the world of matter. It's how thoughts become things. It's how an idea gets from our heads into our hands. While this may seem basic and obvious, think back to how often you have given yourself a resolution for self-improvement, or had a great idea to transform the world, and you *did not write it down*. Be honest: What was the result?

Take the goal of losing weight, for example. The World Health Organization estimates that 10 percent of people worldwide are obese,[3] leading to increased risk of heart disease, strokes, diabetes, and some forms of cancer, the leading causes of preventable death.[4] So a 2008 study funded by the National Institutes of Health recruited nearly 1,700 overweight people to experiment with a new approach to losing weight: *food diaries*.

In addition to education and collaboration, the secret weapon in this approach was keeping a food diary, with participants keeping a list of everything they ate, whether that be on a pad of sticky notes or a digital device. While common sense says that keeping a diary would not result in any meaningful weight loss, the participants found that knowing their food choices would be recorded—*rather than eaten and forgotten*—was a powerful motivator to make better choices. Further, they began to notice *patterns* in their eating that could only be appreciated when they could write them down and take the "meta" view.

The results were astounding. "The more food records people kept, the more weight they lost," said the study's author, Dr. Jack F. Hollis. "Those who kept daily food records lost twice as much weight as those who kept no records. It seems that the simple act of *writing down what you eat* encourages people to consume fewer calories."[5]

I have come to appreciate writing as a powerful and advanced technology, whether we're scribbling it on a notepad or typing it on a keyboard. When we write down our ideas, thoughts, or resolutions, we have a *record*. As Jonah Lehrer put it in his book *Imagine: How Creativity Works*, "There was nothing. Now there is something. It's almost like magic."[6]

Until it's on paper,
It's vapor.

The Book Before the Book

One of the first people to formally develop a plan for treating alcoholics was Dr. Richard R. Peabody.[7] Peabody, you should know, was not a doctor, though he was an alcoholic, which was probably the more important requirement of the two.

Peabody was born in 1892 to one of the most distinguished families in Boston. The Peabodys were wealthy New England bluebloods, well connected with the social elite. He attended Harvard, and married Polly Jacob, who was not only the niece of banking magnate J. P. Morgan Jr. but had received a patent for the modern brassiere. When you're not only connected with the Morgan family but married to the woman who created the bra, life's pretty good.

Unless you're an alcoholic. Peabody's drinking became a habit at Harvard and intensified during his service in World War I. He squandered his wife's inheritance on a shipping business, which failed. He drank more heavily, becoming violent and abusive, until finally his wife left him, taking her brassieres.

A broken man, he began attending meetings at a local church, where he developed his own technique of mind hacking. He eventually achieved sobriety and opened an office to help other alcoholics find sobriety as well; he helped so many, in fact, that they gave him the affectionate nickname "Dr. Peabody." In 1931, he wrote a book titled *The Common Sense of Drinking* that outlined his techniques. The book not only became a best seller, but is a mind hacking classic.

He was one of the first to claim that "once an alcoholic, always an alcoholic," and there's no use in trying to drink more responsibly (despite what the beer commercials tell you). To Peabody, complete sobriety is the only option, and he warns of the dangerous tricks that your mind will play on you as you try to give up drinking. Much of his program involves consciously developing "new habits of thought" that will help mentally gird you when these inevitable temptations arise.

You must overrun the old thought habits with new ones, he says. In a technology analogy appropriate to his time period, he likens the mind to a muddy dirt road that is overrun by the hoofprints of horses and carriages. You can't easily get rid of these mental tracks unless you drive through with a newfangled automobile, creating new tracks. The mind has a similar pliability: what modern researchers call *neuroplasticity*, or the ability to create new neural pathways in the brain.

To accomplish this "changing of the mind," one of the fundamental techniques in Peabody's book is for the recovering alcoholic to *write down the next day's schedule*: every item that he or she wishes to accomplish, including both work and rest. He recommends writing down the day's activities in detail, beginning from the time of arising and continuing until bed at night. Then, at the end of the day, the patient reviews the day's schedule, then plans for tomorrow, again *writing it down*.

The purpose of the schedule is to change a negative loop (drinking, feeling terrible, and so drinking some more) into a positive one (making progress, feeling better, and so making more progress). Note the similarities with Benjamin Franklin's Moral Perfection Project, where he reviewed his progress each day in adhering to his values, writing down whether the day was a success.

One of Peabody's patients gives this testimonial about the virtues of writing down his daily schedule:

> This issuance of small commands to myself and my obedience to
> them rapidly restored my self-respect. Incidentally my efficiency in
> my daily work enormously increased, which increased the respect for
> me of other people. This reacted favorably on my confidence in my-
> self. In other words, by perfectly mechanical means I was enabled to

turn what had been a vicious circle into a beneficent circle. The more pride I was able to take in myself, the less need I had of the rallying effect of alcohol when I went out.[8]

Along the way, Peabody is teaching the alcoholic new habits of thought, cutting new mental grooves in the mind. He is also teaching various concentration and relaxation exercises, positive mental loops, and other techniques similar to the ones you're learning in this book.

The Common Sense of Drinking was a great help to me as I was getting sober. I wasn't the only one: the book also had a profound influence on another man, named Bill Wilson, who went on to help another alcoholic or two.

The Cocktail Napkin

It's a classic Silicon Valley idea: two entrepreneurs are having drinks in a bar, and develop a business model so brilliant that they breathlessly scribble it out on a cocktail napkin. (A second cocktail napkin is usually used to draft up a quick NDA.) The "business on a cocktail napkin" meme is so popular because it boils this truth down to its essence: a good idea can only be developed if you write it down.

In practice, building a successful business is a little more complicated. Still, "writing it down" is a critical and surprisingly complicated discipline, as anyone who has ever tried to write a business plan can tell you.

As an entrepreneur, one of the most influential business books I've read is Michael E. Gerber's *The E-Myth Revisited: Why Most Small Businesses Don't Work and What to Do About It*, which has sold over a million copies worldwide.[9] It outlines what Gerber calls the "Entrepreneurial Myth" that most new businesses are started not by entrepreneurs but by *technicians* who enjoy doing the work and want to work for themselves.

For example, a software developer decides he can make more money working as a hired gun than as a full-time employee, so he starts his own business.

His skill set is programming, and that's what he loves, so he starts out doing all the hands-on programming work himself. As the company grows, however, his bias toward working *in* the business will begin to overshadow what he should be doing: working *on* the business.

What Gerber recommends is for the entrepreneur to think of his or her business like a franchise operation. Imagine it as a fully contained *system*—like Edison's R & D laboratory—that can be used to grow and expand to future locations. You probably know a small business that has stayed in the same place for years, never growing, making just enough for their owners to feed their families. Maybe it's a local restaurant or a neighborhood dry cleaner. If the owner is able to shift his or her mental mind-set from *This is my business* to *This is a* prototype *of my business*, that can make all the difference.

One of the fundamental techniques Gerber recommends is *writing it down*. In other words, looking at every process and system within your business, and making it a replicable process that can be clearly written out, step by step, and put into a training manual that can be used to start a new office or store that is exactly like the original. Thinking in this way causes the entrepreneur to shift out of "working *in* the business" mode and get into "working *on* the business" mode.

Gerber's advice is useful not just for small businesses and start-ups but also for mind hackers. Instead of just working *in* the mind, we are also working *on* the mind. We are looking not just at our thoughts but at the *process* of those thoughts, and how they affect our lives. Just like Gerber's business owners, we must take the time to write down, step by step, what we want our minds to think, or we will be like the business owner who spends her entire life running to stay in the same place.

At my content marketing company, Media Shower, writing things down is what we do: a huge network of talented writers and editors create great content for our clients' websites and blogs. Still, writing down our *business processes* is another matter entirely, and only through constant repetition have we been able to turn this into a healthy habit.

If we're documenting how one of our editors should review a writer's work, for example, we start out by writing down the process on a whiteboard, usually as a simple flowchart. Once we get basic agreement, we write up the process in an online document. The ground rules are:

- **Keep it short.** If it's too long, no one will read it.

- **Keep it simple.** We do this for new employees, so anyone should be able to understand it.

- **Keep it flexible.** Things change, so anyone should be able to edit the document at any time.

At most companies I've seen, the "employee training manual"—if they have one at all—is an enormous three-ring binder, written a decade ago, full of procedures that no one actually follows, locked up in a middle manager's closet under a bowling trophy. At Media Shower, it's a collection of short, simple online documents that can evolve with our business. And when we no longer use a particular document, what do we do? *We delete it.*

The goal in writing things down is not to write *everything* down but to strive for the same level of economy and elegance as a well-written line of code. Scott Ambler, a proponent of agile development, argues that programmers should not focus huge amounts of time on writing documentation for their software but strive for documentation that's "Just Barely Good Enough," or JBGE.[10] This does not mean ineffective or "not very good" but actually "the most effective possible," as documentation that has just enough information is one that most people are actually likely to *read*.

In the spirit of JBGE, I'll shut up now.

Don't get it perfect;
Get it done.

The Two-Week Textbook

On a summer day in 1999, Allen Downey sat down in his office at Colby College and did something radical: he started to write a programming textbook.

There's nothing radical about writing a college textbook, of course, provided you have several years, a team of peer reviewers, and a patient editor. Downey's goal, however, was to get it written before class started . . . *in two weeks*.

"Most textbooks are unreadable, dense, and boring," Downey told me, "thousand-page books with no personality." There were plenty of textbooks available for his introductory course on the Java programming language, for example, but each chapter was typically fifty pages or more, and many students couldn't slog through the reading. Worse, the material was poorly organized: the first few chapters were easy, but "then the trapdoor opened, and students fell through the floor."[11]

"Very predictably, in Chapter 5, I knew the students' heads were going to explode," he remembered. "There was too much, too new, too fast." So, as he furiously developed his own textbook in that fourteen-day marathon, he took a different approach.

"I saw it like foldout bleachers," he explained. "If you've got a difficult concept, it can either be a wall, or you can pull it out to allow the students to jump over it. So if I know there will be a wall in Chapter 5, I can pull some of that material forward, to give them a step up in Chapter 2, then another step in Chapter 3, so when I get to the hard part, they can get over it."

Unbelievably, he finished the book in time for his first class, writing one ten-page chapter a day for thirteen straight days.[12] "Part of that was accumulated frustration," he laughed. "I knew exactly what I wanted by that point, so I could **write it down** very quickly." In the spirit of Just Barely Good Enough, he streamlined each chapter to ten pages, explaining each concept as simply as possible. And because he owned the textbook, he could now focus on making it better.

Each week, he gave his students a quiz on their weekly reading assignment so he could get instant feedback on what was working. "Now I'm running in a tight feedback loop. If the students read Chapter 3, and everybody does well on the reading quiz, then I can move on. If everybody reads Chapter 3 and nobody can do the reading quiz, that tells me instantly there is something wrong with Chapter 3 that I need to fix for the next iteration."

In agile programming, Downey's textbook would be called a "Minimum Viable Product," which, like JBGE, lets us quickly release a product so that we can test, learn, and improve. Compare this with the alternate approach, which we might call "Maximum Perfect Product," i.e., we can only release software that is 100 percent bug-free, we can only write books that have been edited to perfection, and we can only write down personal goals once we have deemed them to be absolutely perfect.

Even with its flaws, Downey found that his textbook was far better than the textbook he had been using, and this "rapid feedback loop" helped him iterate quickly. By the time he had taken two or three classes of students through the book, he had developed something that was working very well. In a beautiful bit of meta-creation, Downey had applied great programming philosophy to his own programming textbook: "Release early, release often, get feedback, and improve."

But that was only one of the things that made Downey's textbook experiment so radical. The other was that *he gave the textbook away for free*. In subsequent years, he developed several textbooks, including *How to Think Like a Computer Scientist*, and distributed them under Richard Stallman's GNU license, which means that readers are free to copy, modify, and distribute them. He started his own publishing company, guided by one simple manifesto: "*Students should read and understand textbooks. That's it.*" [13]

Giving away his work spread it to a worldwide audience: his free textbooks have now been translated into multiple *spoken* languages (French, German, Mandarin, etc.) and adapted for multiple *programming* languages (Ruby, Python, Eiffel, etc.). As his fame grew, the premier technical publisher

O'Reilly Media contracted him to write a new series of textbooks, he received an offer to become a Visiting Scientist at Google, and he's now a professor of computer science at the prestigious Frank W. Olin College of Engineering.

Not bad for a two-week writing rampage.

Concentrate, Then Write

One of the reasons I have been so adamant about writing things down throughout this book is because of the *power* that comes from writing—the magnificent capability we all have of creating something from nothing. With mind hacking, you are like an architect creating a blueprint for your life, and blueprints are only useful if they're actually written down. (That's why they're not called blue*thoughts*.)

Your mind hacking skills will be greatly strengthened by simply writing things down after your daily concentration game, which I trust you have been diligently practicing since Section 1.4. The idea is to spend twenty minutes in concentration, then a few minutes writing your positive loops. It's a total time commitment of less than half an hour.

If you were going to school for an advanced degree, or working on a big new project, you would expect to spend far more than half an hour a day. How much more important is working on your own mind! Far more valuable than learning a new skill or getting a certificate, the time you invest each week in mind hacking is time that will pay off for the rest of your life.

It's never been easier to write things down. You probably carry your phone with you everywhere, which will work, as long as you don't mind mashing tiny screen keys with your meaty, oversized thumbs. You probably also spend most of the workday in front of your computer, another easy way to write things down. Don't overlook the power of the old-school pen and notepad: seeing the pages fill up, day after day, is something you don't get on a digital device.

After you've practiced the concentration game in Section 1.4, turn to the practice sheet in the back of the book and write down your five mental loops from the section Feel, Do, Have, Give, and Be, on p. 111. For example:

```
> I'm free from anxiety, and feeling great.
> I will write a novel with best-selling potential.
> I will own a beach house, which I will share with my
  family and friends.
> I will start a nonprofit to help kids learn to read.
> I'm a dependable mother, wife, and friend.
```

This practice is important, for several reasons. First, **writing things down reminds you of your goals on a regular basis.** It's easy for our minds to get distracted, and this recenters your attention on what you have defined for yourself as most important. Writing down your positive loops cements them into your mind.

The research backs it up: writing things down is more likely to lead to large-scale change. "Certain types of writing have a surprisingly quick and large impact," says psychologist Richard Wiseman in his research-based *59 Seconds: Change Your Life in Under a Minute.* "Expressing gratitude, thinking about a perfect future, and affectionate writing"—techniques you've learned throughout this book—"have been scientifically proven to work, and all they require is a pen, a piece of paper, and a few moments of your time." [14]

We talked about Laura King's studies, in which test subjects were asked to spend time writing about their "best possible future self," and how just a few weeks of this simple exercise led participants to be quantifiably happier and healthier. By writing down your five positive loops from the previous section on a daily basis, after your concentration game, you can experience the same benefit.

Second, **writing things down offers you an opportunity to reflect.** You may find that valuable insights and ideas come to you during your concentration practice; by building in this Edison-like system for capturing them immediately afterward, you're more likely to *do* something with them. Think of it as your internal R&D lab.

Third, **writing things down gives you a chance to improve.** As with Allen Downey's programming textbook, once he had written the initial draft, he could then test it with real students and continue to improve it over time. Many people are frozen by the need to get it perfect, but that's not how great programmers work, and it's not how nature works. In the spirit of Just Barely Good Enough, write it down, and let it evolve.

Most important, **there is incredible, mind-altering power in repetition.** We'll talk more about that power next.

MIND GAME

Write Now

After completing your daily concentration game, write down each of your positive loops on your practice sheet.

[3.2]

<REPEAT>

Scott Adams, the creator of the *Dilbert* comic empire, is one of the most successful cartoonists of our time. In addition to being published in thousands of newspapers worldwide, *Dilbert* has been spun off into several best-selling books, an animated series, and hundreds of *Dilbert*-themed toys and games.[1]

But at one time, Scott Adams was just another midlevel office drone in a large, bureaucratic organization, just like Dilbert.

Adams had always dreamed of becoming a cartoonist: from an early age, he adored Charles Schulz's *Peanuts*, and felt that drawing such a strip would one day be his career. As an adult, however, he found himself working a "number of humiliating and low-paying jobs" in northern California.[2] He was continually looking for a way out so he could make his cartooning dream a reality.

A friend told him about a repetition technique, where you *write down your positive mental loop fifteen times each day*. His friend claimed that it worked for her. "The thing that caught my attention," he related, "is that the process doesn't require any faith or positive thinking to work." Just the act of writing down your loop, she claimed, was enough to make it happen. In the spirit of self-experimentation, and figuring that he had nothing to lose but time, Adams gave it a try.

His first attempt was the straightforward:

> > I, Scott Adams, will become rich.

In his books *The Dilbert Future* and *How to Fail at Almost Everything and Still Win Big*, he tells the story of making two ridiculously lucky stock picks that came to him out of the blue that year.[3] Both were long shots, and both ended up being among the top market stories that year. He sold both stocks immediately, so he wasn't rich, but the odds of an amateur picking two red-hot winners seemed unlikely.

He was less skeptical of the technique, but still not quite a believer. He decided to try the technique on another goal: getting an MBA from University of California at Berkeley. He had already taken the GMAT test that's required for MBA applications, and scored in the 77th percentile: not good enough for UC Berkeley. So he began writing down this positive loop, fifteen times each day:

> > I, Scott Adams, will score in the 94th percentile on the
> > GMAT.

In the weeks leading up to the test, he bought GMAT study books and took plenty of practice tests. Each time he scored at about the 77th percentile. Still, he patiently wrote down his positive loop over and over, fifteen times each day.

The day of the test came. He took the test, feeling that he had scored about the same. He kept up the repetition technique as he waited for the GMAT test scores to arrive in the mail.

Finally, the test results came. He took the envelope out of the mailbox, opened it, and looked at the box he had pictured in his mind so many times before. *He scored in exactly the 94th percentile.* Adams recounts:

> That evening, I sat in a chair with the GMAT results next to me, alternately staring at the wall and then staring at the ninety-four. I kept expecting it to change. It didn't. And that night I knew that nothing would ever be the same for me. Everything I thought I knew about how the Universe was wired was wrong.[4]

After earning his MBA, still working his day job, he began repeating a new loop. Each morning, before he left for work, he would get up at 4:00 a.m. to draw what would eventually become *Dilbert*. He also began to write this positive loop, fifteen times each day:

> I, Scott Adams, will become a syndicated cartoonist.

Despite a number of setbacks and rejections, and through a series of unlikely coincidences and lucky breaks, he eventually became a syndicated cartoonist. In fact, he's arguably the *most* syndicated cartoonist alive today: *Dilbert* is published in 2,000 newspapers worldwide, in 65 countries, and in 25 languages.

With his analytical mind, Adams tried to reverse-engineer why this technique works in his books and in various posts to his blog.[5] While he called his experiences with the repetition technique "fascinating and puzzling" as well as "wonderful and inexplicable," he also was careful not to attribute them to "voodoo or magic." Instead, he theorized about a logical explanation, even acknowledging that it might be nothing more than "selective memory" (perhaps he tried the repetition technique multiple times but only remembered his successes).

Adams points to research done by the psychiatrist Richard Wiseman in which he studied people who described themselves as "lucky." It turns out they didn't have any special powers except for one: they were more likely to notice opportunities. As Adams puts it, "Optimistic people's field of perception is literally greater." If you are methodically repeating your goals each day, you are more likely to notice the people and situations that can help you achieve those goals *as they present themselves*.

In my experience, this is absolutely true. When you repeat your goals daily, *you set your expectations accordingly*, and you begin viewing situations in a different light. If you're repeating your goal of losing weight and someone invites you to a kickboxing class, you see it as an opportunity, not another way to embarrass yourself. If you're repeating your goal of becoming an entrepreneur and they're going through layoffs at your day job, you might see it as an opportunity to take the severance package and strike out on your own.

Adams also points out that repeatedly writing things down takes effort. Because you are investing time and energy in this small goal, you are committing yourself to investing time and energy in your larger goal. It is a way of kick-starting your mind into achieving your dreams, a kind of mental bootstrapping.

"My favorite explanation . . . also has the least evidence to support it," Adams concludes, "i.e., none." In this explanation, reality is so mind-bogglingly complex that our minds simply deliver a "highly simplified illusion that we treat as facts." In this model of reality, the constant repetition of our goals may be a "lever" that we use to create some natural chain of cause and effect, but not a chain we are capable of understanding. So when the results come, by what appears to be luck or coincidence, it is simply by natural laws that are not yet fully understood. "While this view is unlikely to be correct," he admits, "it has the advantage of being totally cool to think about." (It is also similar to the ideas of Plato and *The Matrix*: a deeper reality lies behind this one.)

In the end, Adams's repetition technique is one of the easiest self-experiments you can try: it's totally free, and you have nothing to lose but your time. "Here's a good test of your personality," Adams concludes, in response to the skeptics. "If all of your friends told you that they win money on the slot machines whenever they stick their fingers in their own ears, would you try it? Or would you assume that since there is no obvious reason it could work, it's not worth the effort?"

Repetition is Key

Repetition is key. Also, repetition is key.

One of the best parts about living in Boston, besides the wealth of technology talent, is sledding in the winter. It's a thrill seeker's dream, because you can sled as long as you want, as often as you want, and, unlike roller coasters or hallucinogens, it's *totally free*.

I live near Wellesley College, the renowned all-women's college that has produced notable alumni like Nora Ephron and Hillary Clinton. Wellesley has a sledding hill that is just phenomenally dangerous. It has (what feels like) an 85-degree incline, where you attain (what feels like) speeds of up to 75 miles per hour. On one side of the hill, a fifteen-foot oak branch spreads out across the snow, like a giant, deadly limbo stick. If you don't press your body flat into the sled, *you will be decapitated by the tree*. It's insane that they allow sledding on the hill at all, but even more insane is that the women of Wellesley College sled down the hill on *plastic trays from the dining hall*. (It's funnier if you picture Hillary Clinton on a tray.)

As any sledding enthusiast knows, if you get to the hill after a fresh snow, it's just clean powder. Then, as people sled down the hill, it creates grooves, or tracks, in the snow. After a few days the Wellesley students have built snow ramps and moguls at the bottom, so that sledding down one of these tracks will launch you into orbit.

A few days after a snow, you'll find one set of snow tracks that take you under the Oak Tree of Death, and another set that will shoot you off the Ramps into Hyperspace. Even if you start your sled on another area of the hill, you end up locking into one of those two tracks.

Our minds are like that hill. The constant repetition of our negative loops cuts deep mental grooves, and it's natural for our minds to "lock into" those grooves, even when the negative loops are self-destructive.

The good news is, through repetition, *you can cut a new groove*. When I take my kids sledding at the hill, we often have to cut a new track, packing down the snow where we want it to go, then physically slowing and redirecting ourselves to the new track. The sled "wants" to lock into the existing groove, but by patiently working the new path we can eventually get the sled to lock into the new one instead.

Through the concentration and writing exercises that you're practicing, you're probably already seeing when the mind begins to go down one of those dangerous paths:

> *Everything I do ends in failure/sadness/embarrassment . . .*
> *I'm a terrible parent/partner/friend . . .*
> *I'm no good at exercise/math/romance . . .*
> *I shouldn't have said/done/thought that . . .*
> *I'm fat/lonely/hopeless . . .*

The sled has started down the hill, but if you develop the skill of *noticing* it going down this track, then you can develop the skill of *redirecting* it to a different track, preferably with one of your positive loops.

> *Everything I do ends in failure . . . but hold on. Some things I do are actually quite successful, like the homemade Transformers outfit I built for Comic-Con last year.*

> *I'm a terrible parent . . . but wait a minute. My son gave me a hug yesterday, out of the blue. Like all parents, I have room to improve, but I'm doing something right.*

> *I'm no good at exercise . . . actually, I have been working out twice a week for the last month, so although it still doesn't feel natural, I'm getting better.*

I shouldn't have said that . . . but you know what? I'm probably the only one who will even remember it, and I'm growing more self-confident every day.

I'm lonely . . . but the good news is that I just joined a church, I'm widening my circle of friends, and I'm confident I'll find a loving partner.

You can't force your mind to stop thinking negative thoughts! If I ask you *not* to think of your grandparents making love, for example, it will be virtually impossible to stop yourself, particularly if I ask you not to think of them in the freakiest positions imaginable, with a 1970s disco bass line in the background. What we are after is not mind *control* but mind *training*. The mind will naturally follow the tracks you have laid down for it over the course of your life, but with effort and persistence, you can redirect it into a new groove.

If your goal is not complete,
Lather, rinse, repeat.

With constant repetition, you can eventually perform what I call "mind judo." When an opponent lunges at the judo master, the master effortlessly uses his opponent's natural momentum to throw him off balance. He calmly steps aside and lets the opponent flip himself over. When the mind comes at you with the negative loop, you can use that natural momentum to kick off the positive loop instead.

A drink sure would be nice . . . (flip) . . . except that my sobriety is the foundation of all the good things in my life.

I cannot stand that woman . . . (flip) . . . but I'm free from resentment, and I'm able to live and let live.

I will never get out of debt . . . (flip) . . . but I've already come a long way, and I can do it.

Rather than obsess on the things that cause you pain, the mind can now obsess on the things that bring you peace.

To put it another way: Repetition is key.

Repetition Method #1: The $10 Million Check

The actor Jim Carrey grew up so poor that at one time, his entire family lived in a trailer on a relative's lawn. After school, he would put in eight-hour work-days at a local factory to help support them.[6] His childhood was so difficult that he dropped out of high school and, at age twenty-one, moved to Holly-wood with the dream of escaping his life of poverty and building a successful career as a comedian and performer.

One night after arriving in Hollywood, Carrey made a critical decision that affected the course of his life, a decision that would bring laughter to hundreds of millions of people worldwide. He drove his run-down Toyota up to the Hollywood Hills and parked where he could see the glittering lights of Tinseltown stretched before him like a blanket of dreams. In his mind, he saw himself entertaining the world through TV and movies. And because he wanted a physical reminder of his success, he *wrote it down*.

He took out his checkbook and wrote a check to himself for $10 million, dating it ten years in the future. In the memo field he wrote, "For acting services rendered." He kept the check in his wallet as a constant reminder of his goal. In the years to come, each time he pulled out his wallet to pay for something, there was the check, serving as a visual repetition. As he struggled through failed sitcoms and bad sets at Yuk Yuk's, there was the check. As he took small supporting parts in movies, there was the check. And as his career began to finally take off in the 1990s, there was the check.

There is nothing mysterious about the fact that *a constant reminder of your goal will make you more likely to achieve it*. Through that constant repeti-tion of the check, Carrey stayed focused on his goal of becoming a successful entertainer through the inevitable ups and downs of a Hollywood career. As it turns out, though, Jim Carrey did not exactly achieve his goal. Ten years later, he was not earning $10 million per film; he was earning *$20 million per film*.

Repetition can take many forms. Carrey's technique was what we might call a *reminder repetition*: writing your positive loops somewhere you will see them regularly, like your wallet. The word "re-mind," in fact, literally means *bringing it back to mind*. You are responsible for creating these reminders for yourself! No one else can do it for you. Here are some good places for your reminder repetitions:

- Hanging on your computer monitor

- Nightstand/dresser

- Computer wallpaper

- Screensaver

- Smartphone background

- Breakfast area

- Daily alarm

- Automated email reminder

- In the bathroom (across from the toilet is ideal)

And in case it's a little weird to have your positive loops hanging out for friends and roommates to read, you can always encrypt your loop into a code only you understand, hide it in your passwords, or use a photo that represents your goal. Alternately, you could just not care whether they see it.

As I'm writing this, I'm listening to my white-noise soundtrack, where I have recorded myself reading my positive loops, then mixed them into white noise just below the threshold of hearing. Although the research on subliminal learning has been inconclusive, I don't believe anyone has ever studied the long-term effects of listening to yourself repeating your positive loops thousands of times a day. I'll let you know what I find.

Repetition Method #2: Don't Break the Chain

Software developer Brad Isaac started out his career as a stand-up comic. One night he was performing in the same club as Jerry Seinfeld, at a time when Seinfeld's legendary television sitcom was just starting to take off. Isaac plucked up his courage, approached Seinfeld, and asked if he had any advice for a young struggling comedian.

"DON'T BREAK THE CHAIN," Seinfeld replied.[7]

Seinfeld went on to explain that the way to get better at writing jokes was through *repetition*, so he committed himself to writing a certain number of jokes each day, whether he felt funny or not. After the day's joke writing was complete, he marked a large red X for that day on a wall calendar. (It was Benjamin Franklin's Moral Perfection Project for funny people.)

After a few days, he had a chain. Now the game was to see how long he could go without breaking the chain—without missing a day of writing jokes. Each day, his satisfaction would come from seeing the unbroken chain of red Xs, that constant repetition, knowing he was steadily working toward his goal. If he missed a day, he'd have to start over, and that alone was enough to keep him working on his craft.

Again, there's no mystery in the idea that practicing something makes you better at it—the Seinfeld system just *visualizes* that repetition, so you can challenge yourself to beat your previous record ("I did a two-week chain last time, let's see if I can go for three"). The Mind Hacking app (available at www.mindhacki.ng) also lets you track "chains" of progress—though currently it does not feature a recording of Jerry Seinfeld imploring you, "DON'T BREAK THE CHAIN," which I know would motivate *me*.

Repetition Method #3: Smiling in the Shower

One of the easiest ways to repeat your mental loops is to just *silently recite them to yourself*. This can be an efficient way of using "mental downtime" such as:

- Your daily commute

- Boring meetings

- Waiting in line

- Waiting at stoplights

- Waiting for appointments

- Exercising

- Doing chores (housework, yard work, etc.)

- While you shower (the best possible time, in my opinion)

You can accelerate this technique by repeating the positive loop to yourself, not like a zombie, but with *feeling*. A 2008 study by German psychologist Dr. Fritz Strack showed that smiling actually makes you feel happier.[8] He had two groups of test subjects read a series of Gary Larson's *Far Side* cartoons. One group was instructed to hold a pencil between their *teeth* without touching their lips, and one group holding the pencil between their *lips* but not touching their teeth. Without realizing it, the "teeth" group had their faces contorted into smiles, while the "lips" group had their faces puckered into frowns.

Amazingly, the group that was forced to smile *felt* happier, and found the cartoons funnier, than the group that was forced to frown. Several years later, another study showed that regular smiling will improve other areas of your life, including interacting more positively with others and thinking more optimistically.[9]

By mentally repeating your positive loops to yourself while smiling, you are more likely to view them optimistically and take the positive steps needed to make the required changes in your life. You can even do one better than that by encouraging yourself to *feel* enthusiastic about your positive loops.

Think back to when you felt truly excited or encouraged about a project or event, and try to capture that emotional state as you repeat your mental loop.

Perhaps this sounds like I am encouraging you to become a grinning lunatic, rocking back and forth as you repeat things to yourself on the highway. The difference between the mental repetition technique and OCD is that you are reprogramming the mind, not repeating things out of compulsion or anxiety. You will see the difference, because *it is difficult to do!* It is much easier to turn on a podcast or check your email (our *true* obsessive-compulsive disorders) rather than taking a few moments to calmly repeat your mental loops.

Think of this technique as "Smiling in the Shower" and it really works. "It took years for your mind to build its scaffolding of tricks and worries," says Dr. Joan Borysenko, the Harvard-trained psychologist. "It will take time to dismantle them." [10] And the key to that dismantling is repetition.

Repetition is . . . well, you know.

MIND GAME

Reminding Your Mind

Set up a reminder system for yourself, similar to the ideas in Section 3.2, that will repeatedly bring one of your positive loops to mind:

- Repetition Reminders: The $10 Million Check
- Repetition Trackers: Don't Break the Chain
- Talking to Yourself: Smiling in the Shower

Write down a brief description of your reminder system on your practice sheet.

<SIMULATE>

Nikola Tesla may have been the greatest geek who ever lived.

The Serbian-American inventor was awarded three hundred patents during his lifetime, beginning with electric motors, and eventually encompassing such diverse inventions as ship navigation devices, wireless lighting, and a plane that would take off and land vertically—all in the early 1900s.[1] In harnessing the forces of nature, Tesla seemed almost godlike in his powers: at one of his labs, he generated 135-foot bolts of artificial lightning, creating thunder that could be heard 15 miles away.[2]

Like many great thinkers, some of Tesla's ideas seemed insane for the time, even by today's standards. He had plans for a robot that could operate of its own free will and free countries from war;[3] the saturation of schoolrooms with electric fields to enhance the intelligence of children;[4] and a "death ray" that he boasted could bring down ten thousand enemy airplanes at a distance of two hundred miles.[5]

Because he was a terrific showman, he earned a popular reputation as a "mad scientist," and it was sometimes difficult to know what he had actually invented, what was in development, and what existed only in his mind.

For many years, Tesla tried to perfect a device that could *project your thoughts onto the wall*, an invention he called the "thought camera." As he explained in a newspaper interview late in his life, "In 1893, while engaged in certain investigations, I became convinced that a definite image formed in thought, must . . . produce a corresponding image on the retina, which might be read by a suitable apparatus."[6] His diagram of this device resembled a movie projector, with the operator staring into the machine, which projected his thoughts on the wall. Being able to project your thoughts like a movie, you have to admit, would be both incredibly cool and incredibly disturbing.

The thought camera was a natural fit for Tesla, who from an early age showed an unusual ability to see pictures in his mind. In fact, he was afflicted with a particularly severe form of what today would be called "visual thinking" or "picture thinking." A simple word like "engine" would trigger a vision of the object—a vision so strong that, as he later explained, "Many times it was impossible for me to tell whether the object I saw was real or not."[7] He literally could not tell the difference between his mental pictures and the real world, a handicap that caused him considerable anxiety and discomfort throughout his life.

But this strange curse could also be a blessing: as a child, he was able to do integral calculus in his head, leading his teachers to think he was cheating.[8] As he grew older, he began to gain mastery over the mental pictures, learning to visualize his inventions in great detail before writing down a single word.

His style was a marked contrast with that of Thomas Edison, who was also his boss—and later his archnemesis. Tesla rose to prominence working under Edison, and perhaps it was inevitable that the two great men, with their differing approaches, would eventually become bitter enemies. The animosity began when Edison asked Tesla to redesign his direct current generators; Edison allegedly claimed he would pay Tesla $50,000 for completing the project. When Tesla delivered the goods, the notoriously stingy Edison claimed the offer had been a joke—but as a consolation prize, he would raise Tesla's salary from $10 to $28 per week. Tesla told Edison he could take his generator and shove it.

Tesla went on to develop the alternating current (AC) standard of electricity, which was in direct competition to Edison's direct current (DC) standard. The two men waged a bitter war of public relations and reputations, officially known as the "War of Currents," with Tesla's AC standard eventually winning out. Some biographers believe they both refused a joint Nobel Prize because neither man wanted to share it with the other.

Moreover, their two inventing styles were fundamentally different: Edison, who claimed that "genius is one percent inspiration, ninety-nine percent perspiration," conducted thousands of experiments, meticulously writing down the results of each. Tesla, gifted with the ability to see strikingly vivid mental pictures, worked through problems in his mind, writing down plans only when he had a finished product.

When Edison died in 1931, the *New York Times* ran an extensive retrospective of his life, with tributes from some of the greatest luminaries of the day. The only wet blanket was Tesla, still not letting it go:

> He had no hobby, cared for no sort of amusement of any kind and lived in utter disregard of the most elementary rules of hygiene.

He then wrote these telling words:

> His method was inefficient in the extreme, for an immense ground had to be covered to get anything at all, unless blind chance intervened. At first, I was almost a sorry witness of his doings, knowing that just a little theory and calculation would have saved him 90 percent of the labor.[9]

For Tesla, the key was running **mental simulations**: a detailed picture of exactly what you wanted to achieve, working through all the problems, roadblocks, and obstacles in your mind. For Edison, the key was **writing it**

down: doing the experiments one at a time, working through the problems in real-world conditions.

As we've seen, there's a wealth of research to support Edison's approach. But new studies show that Tesla's method can work for us as well. I propose a hybrid approach, a final reconciliation between these two great minds. In addition to developing Edison's habit of writing it down, you can also increase your Tesla-like powers of mental simulation. Here are three easy methods.

Method #1: Shall We Play a Game?

In the classic 1983 geek movie *WarGames*, a teenage hacker (played by Matthew Broderick) breaks into a high-level military computer that is programmed to run wartime simulations. Thinking it's a game, the hacker accidentally sets off a countdown to total nuclear annihilation of Russia. In the climactic scene, the entire Department of Defense watches breathlessly as the computer runs countless simulations of World War III, all resulting in mass destruction of the planet.

After a dramatic pause, the computer concludes:

```
> A strange game. The only way to win is not to play.
```

A **simulation** is the imagining of a process or system over time. A flight simulator is a virtual environment where pilots can be trained to respond to emergency situations. A simulation game like *SimCity* lets you develop a virtual world and watch how it evolves. There are mathematical simulations, financial simulations, and weather simulations. But most important, there are *mental* simulations.

A mental simulation is simply *imagining how something will play out*. We do this all the time, from *Here's how this conversation will probably go* to *How much money will I have when I retire?* Let's define "simulation" as different from "imagination": whereas we can use imagination to picture *the final goal*, we use simulation to picture *how we'll get there*.

Like imagination, mental simulation is difficult for most of us: trying to picture the road to success is dark and hazy, and the mind keeps getting distracted. It's hard work. The good news is, just as you can develop the skill of imagination, you can also develop the skill of mental simulation.

At least ten research studies have shown that when people are asked to imagine a future scenario (such as your positive loops), then asked to rate the likelihood of attaining that scenario, they believe it's more likely to happen if they have spent time doing mental simulations.[10] In a fantastic UCLA study by Lien Pham and Shelley Taylor, they explain why this is so: mental simulations allow us to realistically plan how we get from Point A to Point B.[11]

In the study, they divided a class of psychology students into three groups. In preparation for an upcoming midterm exam, the researchers asked one group of students to simply *imagine* themselves getting an A: seeing their test score, feeling the satisfaction of a good grade. They asked a second group to run a *mental simulation* of getting an A: where and when they would study, how they would handle the temptation to procrastinate, taking the exam itself, *then* the final test score and rush of good feeling. A third group acted as a control, simply monitoring their study habits each day.

The first group of students, who mentally *pictured* a good grade for five minutes each day, scored about the same as the control group. The second group, who mentally *simulated* the process of getting to a good grade for five minutes a day, scored eight points higher: a full letter grade! The researchers concluded that, by itself, "visualizing success" decreases our motivation to actually *do the work that leads to success*. Students who ran mental simulations, on the other hand, showed better planning skills and less anxiety at test time. (Put that way, the findings seem like common sense!)

The takeaway is that if your positive loop is to become an award-winning playwright, you don't just see your name on a Broadway marquee. Instead, you picture the act of writing a script, finding financial backers, working with the cast and crew in rehearsals, solving production problems, and doing interviews and publicity, with your name on the marquee a *result* of the mental simulation you've just run.

If you are trying to get free from addiction, you can think through the *process* of asking for help, going to twelve-step meetings, building a network of sober friends, all while you get stronger and happier. You can simulate situations where you are likely to run into problems: parties, or family reunions, or New Year's Eve, and how you successfully navigate those temptations.

If your goal is to find a cure for cancer, you can run a mental simulation—a mind movie—of going through years of training and education, countless hours of research, making critical partnerships and collaborations, making the crucial insights and discoveries, then the clinical trials and, finally, success. You can see your name in Wikipedia, but only as the result of the simulation.

Here's how Jack Nicklaus, widely regarded as the greatest professional golfer of all time, described his approach:

> Before every shot I go to the movies inside my head. Here is what I see. First, I see the ball where I want it to finish, nice and white and sitting up high on the bright green grass. Then, I see the ball going there; its path and trajectory and even its behavior on landing. The next scene shows me making the kind of swing that will turn the previous image into reality. These home movies are a key to my concentration and to my positive approach to every shot.[12]

Nicklaus used a "reverse simulation," starting with the end goal and working backward to the present moment. Either method is fine: you can tell the story forward or backward. The important thing is that you *tell the story*.

This is important, because there *will* be a story. If you're trying to become a millionaire, a Brink's truck is probably not going to back up to your cellar door and unload cash and gold bullion (although that *would* be an amazing story). It will happen in incremental steps—and by mentally rehearsing, or simulating, the story, you can more clearly see the steps you need to take next.

Will your future play out exactly according to your simulation? We can say with almost total certainty that it will not. Unexpected challenges will present themselves, obstacles you never could have foreseen will block your way. But you will be better equipped to deal with an unpredictable future, because by developing the skill of mental simulation, you can run new simulations in real time, taking the new situation as a starting point.

To simulate reminds
And stimulates your mind.

By repeating your positive loops, you have a powerful new tool to help make them a reality: *mental simulation*. Work these simulations into your daily routine, thinking through all the problems that could arise, and how you will successfully overcome each of them on your way toward your goal. Just as a good computer simulation introduces many random variables, try to predict the unpredictable, and let your mind show you how you will succeed.

You can direct the "mind movie" to a happy ending.

Method #2: Block and Tackle

"I truly believe . . . that your positive mind-set gives you a more hopeful outlook, and belief that you **can** do something great means you **will** do something great."

—Russell Wilson, Seattle Seahawks quarterback

The Seattle Seahawks had a weird idea: to make a kinder, gentler football team.

The story starts with head coach Pete Carroll, a positive, energetic leader who made his way up through the world of college football, rising to lead the New England Patriots to a division title in 1997. After the Patriots failed to even make the playoffs over the next two years, however, Carroll was unceremoniously fired, in what ESPN called a high-profile NFL "flameout." [13] Stung by the experience, Carroll hunkered down in the world of college football for nearly a decade, until he was hired by the Seahawks for the 2010 season.

He was back in the big league, and this time he was determined to do things differently. Carroll had an unusual plan in mind for the Seahawks, one that would make *mental* training every bit as important as *physical* training. He met with Dr. Michael Gervais, a sports psychologist who specialized in "high-stakes environments," where split-second decisions can make the difference between a game-winning play and a life-threatening injury.[14] After their first dinner together, Carroll leaned over to Gervais and said, "What do you say we build a masterpiece together?" And that they did.

The two men created a remarkable program of mind hacking for the Seahawks, utilizing the same skills you're learning in this book: daily concentration exercises, constant repetition of positive loops, and regular mental simulations. In fact, as he explains, simulations are central for success.

"Let's articulate what it feels like," Gervais tells athletes, "when you're at your best." They first imagine, in vivid detail, situations where the athlete was at peak performance. In one-on-one simulation sessions, they make strategies for getting back to that state of peak performance, even in high-stress situations. "We don't talk about winning, or being in the zone: those are after-effects," Gervais explains. "We ask, '*What's getting in the way of you being in an ideal mind-set?*' And we figure out strategies to work through that."[15]

By running countless mental simulations, the players prepare for those critical moments in which games are won or lost: moments of fear. He points out that professional football players are under constant and intense stress: not just the *physical* stress of constant battering and the threat of injury, but the *mental* stress of making a bad play and losing a game, or a championship, or a career. The press ripping you to shreds, the fans tearing you apart, and the enormous sums of money won and lost on a game.

Simulations help them prepare for that moment of indecision and fear, so they can calmly and effortlessly know their next move, rather than being overwhelmed by the stress. If you've ever panicked or frozen up at a public speaking engagement, after being confronted by an angry colleague, or in a moment of high-stakes stress, you can see the practical value of this kind of mental simulation. It's not just for professional athletes, but also for professional mind hackers.

Gervais likens the simulation process to developing mental "tools," but I prefer the analogy of mental "functions." In programming, a function is a block of code that performs a specific function for you: give it an input like "September 1, 2098," and it will return a day of the week, like "Monday." The code is nicely bundled in a neat package, like a little machine into which you feed an input (like the number 25) and it returns an output (like the square root of 25).

Running mental *simulations* is a way of developing these mental *functions*, so that when we find ourselves confronted with difficult situations, we are better equipped to handle them. "We need to get a platform in place," says Gervais, "that allows fear to be part of it, to be comfortable with it, even to have fun with it, and that allows us to master it. That's how to thrive in situations we're not proficient in. *Fear is really central to what we do.*"

In those moments, he goes on to explain, "there is no pressure. It's the moment. And being lost in the moment is so rewarding and so engaging, people become so interested in that moment, that we don't have to challenge them. They become naturally interested. Asking, 'What is it like to be your best?' gets them there."

Seahawks offensive tackle Russell Okung echoes this idea. "It's about quieting your mind and getting into certain states where everything outside of you doesn't matter in that moment. There are so many things telling you that you can't do something, but you take those thoughts captive, take power over them and change them."

You can accelerate the performance of your mental simulations by specifically thinking through *how you will overcome difficulties*: not just "thinking positive" but also "working through the negative." Returning to the analogy of computer functions, given an input (you don't make the sales quota, your kids get caught drinking, your speech is a disaster), what will be the output? In other words, *how will you successfully respond?*

In a 2001 research study, students were asked to identify a large goal, such as going to medical school or becoming an actor. The researchers asked one group of students to think through *positive* benefits of the goal (respect or personal fulfillment), another group to think through *negative* difficulties they were likely to encounter (taking the MCATs or enduring humiliating auditions), and a third group to think through both.[16]

They found the third approach provided the best of both worlds: students who simulated both the outcome, *as well as overcoming the potential difficulties*, achieved more. Additional studies have shown that this two-pronged approach—asking "What's it like to be your best?" as well as "How will you respond in a moment of challenge?"—has proven effective at improving performance for professionals as diverse as nurses, employees, and managers.[17]

In fact, this "difficulty simulation" approach can also be effective for treating depression: instead of obsessing on a negative mental loop (*My family doesn't love me*), patients can start reinvesting mental energy in the higher-order positive loops (*My goal is to feel love and happiness*), and develop alternate ways of getting there.[18] Let's call this the "Block and Tackle" method, where you simulate difficulties in your plan, and how you will successfully overcome them.

The best part of the Seahawks story is its ending: in 2014, Carroll and Gervais led the team to its first-ever Super Bowl victory. The Seahawks trounced the Denver Broncos, 43–8, in one of the largest point spreads in Super Bowl history. Carroll was sixty-two years old, the third-oldest coach to win the championship. But perhaps it's premature to call this the end of the story, since one of the team's positive loops is *Win multiple Super Bowls.*

Method #3: Self-Simulation

There's a final hack for running effective mental simulations: *Imagine yourself in the third person.*

When I'm preparing for a speech, I don't see it through my own eyes, looking out at the audience. I simulate it from the *audience* point of view, as others would see me. I hear it and feel it like I want others to hear it and feel it. In other words, instead of imagining yourself from the first-person or virtual reality POV, it's more effective to see yourself as *others* would see you, like a movie, with you in the starring role.

In a study by Lisa Libby from Ohio State University, the researchers called one hundred registered voters the day before the 2004 U.S. presidential election. They asked each of their test subjects to mentally simulate driving to their local polling location, standing in line, filling out the ballot, and turning it in. For half the group, they instructed them to see themselves voting from the first-person perspective (like an extremely boring version of *Halo*), and the other half from the third-person perspective (like C-SPAN).

When the researchers followed up after the election, they found just over 70 percent of the first-person group went to the polls, while a whopping *90 percent* of the third-person group followed through and voted.[19] It may be that third-person mental simulations have a stronger impact on your self-perception, making you more likely to follow through in the real world. Or it may be that seeing yourself in the "mind movie" encourages a higher-order level of thinking. However it works, it's one more protip I hope you'll find useful.

MIND GAME

The Simulator

After completing your daily concentration game and writing down your positive loops, spend sixty seconds doing a mental simulation on one of these loops, using one of the techniques mentioned here:

- Shall We Play a Game: simulating the steps involved with getting to your goal
- Block and Tackle: simulating specific difficulties and how you will overcome them
- Self-Simulation: seeing yourself in the third person

Check off the day's simulation on your practice sheet.

So far in *Mind Hacking*, we've focused almost exclusively on our own minds. All the tools and techniques we've learned, however, have been in preparation for the final two sections, in which we show how to actively make change in the "real" world. What is the mysterious process by which all this mind hacking alters reality?

Now that our minds are humming like a Cray supercomputer, it's time to connect them with the minds of others. If you think one computer is powerful, imagine what it can do when it's hooked up to the cloud.

<COLLABORATE>

The first version of Wikipedia was a failure.

Jimmy Wales was a web entrepreneur who had found modest success with an online content company called Bomis. Wales had a lifelong interest in knowledge—as a child, he pored over *Brittanicas* and *World Book Encyclopedias*—and he funneled some of the Bomis cash into a far more ambitious enterprise: a comprehensive online encyclopedia called Nupedia.

He hired his friend Larry Sanger as editor in chief of Nupedia. Wales and Sanger had met on a discussion forum, where they debated the philosophy of Ayn Rand (Wales was a fan, Sanger was not). The two men had something of the "odd couple" dynamic of Steve Jobs and Steve Wozniak: Wales was the hard-driving entrepreneur who majored in finance and worked briefly at an options trading firm. Sanger was a doughy, balding academic who had a PhD in philosophy and played the violin.

Wales was largely hands-off: it was Sanger who

made all the countless day-to-day decisions, including how Nupedia would be set up. Sanger's specialty was *epistemology*, the study of knowledge, and he came from the academic community, with its peer review systems and high standards of quality. As he designed the online encyclopedia, his challenge was to allow *online collaboration* in a way that still maintained *overall quality*.

Nupedia, he decided, would be written by volunteers. But unlike Wikipedia, which lets anyone create or edit an article, Nupedia would only accept volunteers who were scholars or subject-matter experts, greatly limiting the available pool of writers. Moreover, Nupedia had a *seven-step review process* before an article would be accepted. Each submission was reviewed by professional editors—preferably with a PhD—before a page could be published.

This painstaking peer review process was meant to ensure that only facts made it through the filter: they were competing, after all, with esteemed reference sources like the *Encyclopedia Britannica*, legendary for their quality and attention to detail. The approval process was *so* tedious and slow, however, that in the three years of its existence Nupedia only published *twenty-five approved articles*.

After a year, Sanger and Wales were frustrated with the lack of progress. When they learned about wikis—online documents that anyone could create or edit—they launched a wiki version of Nupedia, which they originally thought would simply help people create "rough drafts" for Nupedia. The Nupedia community of professional academics recoiled at the idea of collaborating with the masses: an encyclopedia that would let *anyone* submit content? *Without a degree?*

So Sanger created a separate domain, Wikipedia.com (the .org would come later), and sent out his now-famous request to the Nupedia discussion list. "Humor me," he said. "Go there and add a little article. It will take all of five or ten minutes."[1]

While many of the Nupedia contributors refused to participate in the collaborative experiment, others did. It launched in January 2001, and within days, Wikipedia had published more articles than Nupedia. By the end of January, the site had six hundred articles; by March, that number had doubled; by May, it had doubled again. By the end of its first year, users had created over *twenty thousand encyclopedia entries*. Thanks to its "radical collaboration," Wikipedia went into hypergrowth mode, while Nupedia was eventually shut down with its original twenty-five well-researched articles.

Sanger is, in my mind, the unsung hero of the Wikipedia story. Wales will likely be remembered as the founder of Wikipedia, but Sanger did all the heavy lifting, handling the countless political problems of managing an online community. (If you've never done it yourself, it's like childbirth: you can't imagine it unless you go through it.) Reflecting on the success of Wikipedia, Sanger observed:

> Radical collaboration, in which (in principle) anyone can edit any part of anyone else's work, is one of the great innovations of the open source software movement. On Wikipedia, radical collaboration made it possible for work to move forward on all fronts at the same time, to avoid the big bottleneck that is the individual author, and to burnish articles on popular topics to a fine luster.[2]

In other words, this **radical collaboration** not only allowed more pages to be created, it allowed more people to work on them, for a longer period of time. Articles could be polished in public, rather than only publishing when perfect. It's difficult to appreciate now how *utterly counterintuitive* it is to allow rough drafts to be published in a definitive reference work like an encyclopedia. But Sanger says this "early collaboration" was also critical to Wikipedia's success:

> We encouraged putting up their unfinished drafts—as long as they were at least roughly correct—with the idea that they can only improve if there are others collaborating. This is a classic principle of open source software. It helped get Wikipedia started and helped keep it moving. This is why so many original drafts of Wikipedia

articles were basically garbage . . . and also why it is surprising to the uninitiated that many articles have turned out very well indeed.[3]

The great irony of collaboration is that although geeks have created some of the most amazing global collaboration projects in history (Wikipedia, Linux, the Web), we are notoriously bad at collaborating in real life. Many of us are comfortable collaborating with strangers as long as they reside safely behind a screen, accessible only in text format. Some of us not even that!

A computer by itself is powerful, but connected to other computers it becomes far more powerful. The same is true of our minds: they become even more powerful when we connect with like minds. The technical term for this is **network effect**, where a technology becomes more useful as others adopt it. The classic example is the telephone: kind of useful if a few people own one, but *incredibly* useful if everyone owns one. In fact, with each successive person who buys a telephone, *everyone's* telephone becomes more useful.

Wikipedia is a classic example of the network effect: the more people collaborate on articles, the more articles get created, and the more people are attracted to write even more articles. When we look at the incredible scale that websites and mobile apps are now able to achieve, and how rapidly they are able to do so, it is because of the network effects that come from millions of people using them. Success breeds success.

With mind hacking, the more we consciously connect our minds with the minds of others, the more we achieve these powerful network effects. We *amplify* the power of our own minds. I believe this explains why certain moments in history are marked by a clustering of unusually great minds (Socrates, Aristotle, and Plato in ancient Greece; Albert Einstein, Niels Bohr, and Werner Heisenberg in the 1920s and 1930s): the collective power of great minds can literally transform the world.

For the rest of us, it's not just a "nice to have," it is *necessary* to achieving our goals, to making our positive loops a reality. The good news is, the personal rewards that come from collaboration—from working with others, *especially in person*—are enormous. Since collaboration can feel so unnatural for geeks, this chapter focuses on specific things you can do to build collaboration into your life, turbocharging your mind hacking efforts by plugging into the cloud.

Alienus Non Diutius

Steve Jobs wanted Pixar to have one set of bathrooms.

Flush with cash from Pixar's IPO in the late 1990s, Jobs set about designing a sprawling campus for his cutting-edge animation studio. He hired Bohlin Cywinski Jackson, the architectural firm that designed many of the flagship Apple stores, and personally oversaw many of the details, with his legendary flair for micromanagement.[4]

The original design called for three buildings. The first building would contain the computer geeks, the second would contain the animators, and the third would contain everyone else: directors, editors, admin, and so forth. From his previous experience running Apple and NeXT, Jobs understood the value of collaboration. In order to make great movies, he needed the mixing of great minds. Separating teams by discipline was the wrong way to go; he wanted a building that had collaboration *built in*.

His idea was for all three buildings (geeks, arts, and admin) to be connected by an enormous central atrium. Then he looked for a way to force people to use it. First he moved all the mailboxes to the atrium, then the cafeteria and coffee bar. But that still wasn't enough: he wanted Pixar to have just *one set of bathrooms*, located off the atrium.

The idea was to create more great ideas. Jobs believed the forced mingling of people from different disciplines was the way to raise everyone's work to a higher level. Chief creative officer John Lasseter, one of the great creative and technical geniuses of our time, described it like this: "Technology inspires art, and art challenges the technology."[5] Making directors and developers share the same bathroom was a crazy way to force collaboration.

As it turns out, it was a little *too* crazy. Some people would have to walk fifteen minutes to use the toilet, which may have resulted in employees having to make emergency trips to the janitor's sink. Personally, I don't want *any* coworkers nearby: my perfect workplace bathroom would be in a private underground bunker several miles beneath the earth's crust.

You can imagine Jobs ranting like a lunatic, screaming about his centralized bathrooms, while some poor architect tried to get him to compromise. Eventually Jobs got his atrium, but he did have to concede to a few additional bathrooms so those with weak bladders would not wet themselves at work.

The idea of a central collaborative space worked. In an industry where inconsistency is the norm—some movies are hits, some are flops, and most are somewhere in between—Pixar has churned out consistently excellent films, one after another, to the delight of moviegoers and critics alike. The average Rotten Tomatoes score for *all* movies is about 50 percent; the average score for *Pixar* movies is 88 percent (and that number goes up to 93 percent if you leave out *Cars 2*).[6]

Many of us have to force ourselves to collaborate. While technology makes it easier than ever to isolate ourselves, becoming lost in our screens even when we're sitting across the table from each other, technology also makes it easier than ever to connect. Joining discussion groups and online forums where we can collaborate with others who are trying to achieve the same goals is a good first step, but it's even more powerful to do it in person. Here are a few easy ways to build collaboration into your life.

- **Local meetups.** There are other people near you, right now, trying to accomplish the same goals. Do a search for "entrepreneur networking" or "weight loss groups" or "local salmon farming classes," and unless you are living on the International Space Station, you'll find a group meeting near you. Be brave! Put it into your calendar and make the time to go. If I'm wrong and there is no group near you, *start your own*. The Web Innovators Group started as an informal gathering of a dozen people in 1995, and it is now one of the largest technology networking groups in Boston, drawing a thousand magnificent minds together in a huge, sweaty hotel ballroom.

- **Shared workspaces.** If you work from home or by yourself, consider using a coworking office instead, where you can bump into knowledge workers from other industries, giving you fresh perspectives and new ideas. Shared workspaces are cropping up in every major city: they're comfortable, affordable, with unlimited coffee. I'm writing this from the Writers' Loft, a shared space outside Boston started by my friend Heather Kelly. Writing around other writers means I get more quality writing accomplished here than anywhere else.

- **Lunches.** Make it a habit to invite potential collaborators to lunch. Mix it up: Ask different people with different backgrounds. I once worked with a group of IT admins who ate together at the same burrito place every day. They were like gang members, except their turf was Qdoba, with goatees instead of guns. They were also terrible IT admins; trying to get help with a support ticket was like trying to negotiate a Middle East peace accord. I often thought that if they had to eat lunch with people from other departments, they'd be better at their jobs. Meals let us connect with other minds in a pleasurable setting, because everyone loves to eat. Especially IT professionals.

We can't expect collaboration to come to us. As with Pixar, we have to design our lives so that collaboration can naturally happen. The ideas above are just meant to get you started, but if you keep your eyes open, you'll find other ways that collaborative opportunities will naturally present themselves. *Take advantage of them.*

Darla Anderson, an executive producer on Pixar blockbusters like *Monsters, Inc.* and *Toy Story 3*, says, "Part of my job [as a producer] is to make sure everyone is smooshing together. If I don't see lots of smooshing, I get worried."[7] Pixar has mastered the art of smooshing, and your mind hacking efforts will be greatly strengthened by adding more smoosh to your schedule.

At Pixar University, the company's in-house training and development division, a Latin crest hangs on the wall. Around a cartoon drawing of a three-eyed alien in a cap and gown reads the motto *Alienus Non Diutius*. Translated, it reads "Alone No Longer."

Me and My Homebrews

If you lived in Menlo Park, California, in the late 1970s, you may have seen the following advertisement pinned to a community bulletin board at your local library:

> Are you building your own computer? If so, you might like to come to a gathering of people with like-minded interests. Exchange information, swap ideas, help work on a project, whatever.[8]

On the scale of world-changing historical documents, this does not seem quite as profound as the Magna Carta or the Declaration of Independence, neither of which end with the word "whatever." But what emerged from that simple advertisement may end up shaking up history in an even bigger way.

The Homebrew Computer Club was started in 1975 by Gordon French and Fred Moore, geeks ahead of their time. The first meeting was held, appropriately enough, in French's garage. At the first meeting, they breathlessly unveiled the new MITS Altair 8800 microcomputer, a build-it-yourself computer that kicked off the microcomputer revolution. "After my first meeting," Steve Wozniak later recalled, "I started designing the computer that would later be known as the Apple I. It was that inspiring."[9]

As the Homebrew Computer Club grew, it moved to the Stanford Linear Accelerator Center, but the real action would happen afterward, in the informal "swap meets" held in the parking lot of a local Safeway.[10] It was mind-melding collaboration that rocked the nation: Adam Osborne (who founded Osborne Computer Corporation), Jerry Lawson (who created the first cartridge-based video game system), and the legendary phone phreaker John Draper.

These were our founding geekfathers, all hanging out next to the Safeway, and it is impossible to overstate their importance to the Digital Revolution: out of this group came the earliest versions of the hardware, software, and operating systems that power our devices today. Even more significantly, this group was the kernel of what we now call Silicon Valley and the prototype for its culture of openness and collaboration. And it all came out of that humble invitation to "exchange information, swap ideas, whatever."

Ideas are a funny thing: they're more powerful when they're shared. Thomas Jefferson recognized this when he said, "That ideas should freely spread from one to another over the globe, for the moral and mutual instruction of man, and improvement of his condition, seems to have been peculiarly and benevolently designed by nature."

The economist Paul Romer argues that this is because ideas, like telephones, have network effects: the more they're shared, the more useful they become. "When we share objects, we make them less valuable," he observes in Jonah Lehrer's *Imagine: How Creativity Works.* "You don't pay as much for a used car because it's already been used. But ideas don't work like that. We can share ideas without devaluing them. There is no inherent scarcity." Ideas are not only infinite, but the more we share them, the more valuable they become.

"That is why places that facilitate idea sharing tend to become more productive and innovative than those that don't," Romer continues. "Because when ideas are shared, the possibilities do not add up. *They multiply.*"[11] This explains why Silicon Valley is such a hotbed of innovation, with its culture of sharing ideas in Safeway parking lots. It explains why Boston, with over one hundred colleges and universities, is a vast hub of innovation: to get great ideas, just add students and shake.

My favorite example of the power of collaboration is Tel Aviv, which has one of the hottest technology start-up scenes in the world. During a recent visit to Israel, I asked one of our Israeli clients how their relatively small country turns out so many great companies. He pointed out that, in Israel, military service is mandatory for all young people. This means you are, in Pixar's words, "smooshed together" with people from different backgrounds and social classes, and forced to rapidly exchange information to solve problems: a college student could find herself leading a squadron into a simulated battle.

This situation not only kick-starts kids into maturing more quickly, it also helps them develop problem-solving skills based on rapid collaboration. You learn to depend on your team, to share information, and to help make your own ideas better—all fantastic skills for starting a technology business.

Sharing ideas makes them better. "As long as there is spillover between minds," says author Steven Johnson in *Where Good Ideas Come From*, "useful innovations will be more likely to appear and spread. It's not that the network itself is smart; it's that *the individuals get smarter because they're connected to the network.*" [12]

By collaborating, we give our *ideas* new ways to connect. Whether it's in a supermarket parking lot, a conference room, or an auditorium, when we meet like-minded minds, we can "exchange information, swap ideas, help work on a project," or indeed, "whatever."

Helping Others Helps Yourself

The next best decision I made, after the decision to get sober, was to call my friend Mike.

Mike was a recovering alcoholic, and I confess I was scared to call him. If I told no one I was getting sober, only my wife and I would know if I failed. But telling Mike was another story: now I had another person who knew my intention.

I'm not sure what I expected from Mike. Maybe a sympathetic ear, or a few words of encouragement. But Mike took the bull by the horns. "Good for you," he said. "There's a meeting tonight. Let's go."

Mike not only got me involved with twelve-step programs, but he was brutally honest that I needed to practice *helping other people*. His advice was all the more powerful because Mike spends a significant amount of his time helping other recovering alcoholics: speaking at halfway houses, rehab centers, and church basements across New England. He's like the Mother Teresa of alcoholics, if Mother Teresa had a crew cut and spoke with a Boston accent.

This form of collaboration—helping each other get and stay sober—is a tradition among recovering alcoholics. I could call Mike at any time of the day or night, and he would be there; what's more, he regularly reached out to *me*. I have a hard enough time answering text messages from my own mother, so the sacrifices that Mike makes to help others is incredibly inspiring, and gives you hope for the human race. And there are many others just like Mike, an anonymous underground of help and support.

Even if you're not trying to get free of addiction, helping other people is still a particularly powerful form of collaboration. *When you help other people, you're also helping yourself.* For example, when you teach something, you also **deepen your own understanding**, which is why I encouraged you to teach the concepts of mind hacking at the beginning of this book. Teaching makes us define and articulate a subject; even when you think you know it, you don't *really* know it until you've explained it to someone else.

Helping other people also **makes you accountable**. If you are helping someone else get sober, you are putting yourself in a position where you don't want to let the other person down. It strengthens your resolve to stay sober yourself, as you're now the role model! Without question, one of the best things about being a parent is that it has made me a better person. I strive to live a life that is worthy of being emulated, since I know my personal example is likely the biggest help I can give my children.

When you help other people, you also **alter your self-concept**. You slowly move from "a drunk who gets drunk" to "a recovering alcoholic who helps alcoholics to recover." With mind hacking, we're trying to change who we are, and nothing changes us more quickly than *playing the part*. If we're trying to stay sober, it's hugely beneficial to serve in a role where we *have* to stay sober.

These benefits come to you, no matter what you're trying to achieve with mind hacking. Look for opportunities to collaborate *where you can actively help others*. If you're trying to start a business, get involved with an entrepreneurial networking group. If you're trying to lose weight, try weight-loss support groups like Weight Watchers. If you're trying to develop the next killer app, attend mobile developer meetups. And always with the spirit of *service*: not *What will I get out of this?* but *What can I give to this?*

When getting my MBA, one of my favorite classes was called Leadership and Influence. In that class, I learned the powerful concept of *reciprocity*, the idea that if I do something nice for you, you will be favorably disposed to do something nice for me. This is why we write thank-you notes, and why we feel awkward when someone gives us a holiday gift and we don't have a gift in return. It's deeply embedded in our society, possibly even in our biology.

You know the "mystery box" in certain video games that will reward you with some mystery surprise? Maybe it's a power-up, or bonus coins, or even an extra life. Every time we help someone else, it's like dropping a mystery box that will later bring us some small unexpected reward. Helping people makes them want to help you.

Even though it's called mind hacking, we can't keep it all in our minds. We've got to collaborate, because helping others helps ourselves.

MIND GAME

Share the Dream

Share one of your positive loops with someone else: a friend, relative, or other trusted confidant. Be brave! Research shows that sharing your goals with someone else makes you more likely to achieve them.[13]

Write down this person's name on the practice sheet at the end of the book.

You're Soaking in It

The mind hacking program is open source because we *want* it to be collaborative. But radical collaboration, like the kind that fueled Wikipedia, is radically scary. If you think it was an easy decision to post this entire book online, months before *Mind Hacking* was available in stores, you'd be wrong. Traditional publishing wisdom says that this is crazy, but I credit my publisher for having the courage to try something new. ("Times were tough growing up," my editor Jeremie likes to joke. "My father was a door-to-door Wikipedia salesman.")

Crowdsourcing the book, however, has made it so much better. (The first version, for example, was written using only vowels.) We've had thousands of people read *Mind Hacking*, and they've given us feedback ranging from typos and fact checks to major structural changes. Like Allen Downey's programming textbook, this has let us quickly iterate and test new versions of the book, seeing where people get "stuck" and pulling the difficult material forward, like Downey's analogy of pull-out bleachers.

The takeaway: Don't collaborate halfheartedly; strive for *radical* collaboration. Swallow your pride, take the attitude of a student, and just *get yourself out there*. Stretch yourself! You'll learn all kinds of surprising things when you connect with other people, like what you thought would be obvious often needs extra explanation.

For example, by far the most common question we've received from our test readers is "Do you mind if I share *Mind Hacking*? I know someone who *really* needs to read this book."

So, for the record: YES! Please share this book!

For heaven's sake,
Collaborate!

<ACT>

Whether You Wish to Model a Flower in Wax;
to Serve a Relish for Breakfast or Supper;
to Plan a Dinner for a Large Party or a Small One;
to Cure a Headache;
to Bury a Relative;
Whatever You May Wish to Do, Make, or to Enjoy,
Provided Your Desire has Relation to the Necessities of Domestic Life,
I Hope You will not Fail to 'Enquire Within.'
   — Editor's Introduction, *Enquire Within upon Everything*[1]

In the mid-1800s, *Enquire Within upon Everything* was a popular encyclopedia found in many Victorian homes. It covered everything a modern family could possibly need to know, from the rules of etiquette to drafting a will. The first editions contained thousands of concise instructions on problems like getting rid of the bad smell in a freshly painted room (burn a handful of juniper berries) to how to administer an opium enema (three grains of opium, two ounces of starch, two ounces of warm water, then pass out).

You can imagine a bright, curious child being

absolutely spellbound by such a treasure trove of information, particularly before the invention of screens. Young Tim Berners-Lee, growing up in England in the 1960s, was lucky enough to have a copy of *Enquire Within* in his household, and he spent hours poring over its how-to instructions on parlor games, natural remedies, and household tips. There was something inspiring about this massive collection of random advice presented in a coherent structure.

After graduating from Oxford in the 1970s with a degree in physics, Berners-Lee landed a contract job at CERN, the mother of all physics labs. In his research, he repeatedly found himself frustrated by needing some small bit of information that his mind refused to serve up, and his thoughts would frequently drift back to *Enquire Within upon Everything*. If only there was a way to present *all* the world's information in some readily available format, so you could instantly pull up any random fact you needed!

This was the vision that formed in his mind—all the world's information, readily accessible—but it was only the first part of the vision. The second part was that, by getting all the information into computers, we could then use computers to help us crunch all that information. Once all the information was catalogued—*all* the information—computers could show us how to make our work more efficient, our relations more peaceful, our lives better.

Berners-Lee didn't just sit around dreaming: he made a decision to **act**. His first attempt was a simple program that had pages of information called "cards," and hyperlinks between the cards.[2] This system served two purposes: it let him share his projects with other CERN research scientists, but it also allowed him to easily access their projects. It was collaboration in action. Thinking back to the Victorian reference guide, he called the program ENQUIRE.

ENQUIRE, like Nupedia, was ultimately not a success: it wasn't open enough. There were constraints around the types of information that could be linked, which turned out to be a deal breaker. "One had to be able to jump from software documentation to a list of people to a phone book to an organizational chart to whatever," Berners-Lee recalled, once again invoking the mysteriously prophetic word "whatever."[3]

But Rome wasn't built in a day, and neither was the Web. Berners-Lee took a job at a computer company, honed his networking skills, then returned to CERN in the 1980s. By the end of the decade he was ready to act again. This time, all the pieces were in place.

CERN was now the largest node on the Internet, and the sheer volume of information at CERN was staggering. Some easy way of cataloging all that information was desperately needed. A number of technologies had been invented to facilitate the sharing of this information, but what Berners-Lee did was to put them together. "I just had to take the hypertext idea and connect it to the Transmission Control Protocol and domain name system ideas and— ta-da!—the World Wide Web."[4]

Although he makes it sound like an act of magic, nothing could be further from the truth. It was actually a series of carefully planned **actions**, of goals and subgoals, of problems and solutions, before the inventor of the World Wide Web was able to invent the World Wide Web.

First, he had to convince his boss to let him work on it, so in 1989 he wrote a proposal. With the dead-sexy name of "Information Management: A Proposal," the proposal was accompanied by a diagram that looked like a schizophrenic Christmas present: a collection of boxes, clouds, and lines interconnected in a flowchart from hell. It's no wonder that the proposal was rejected—although, in Berners-Lee's defense, how would you *possibly* illustrate the Web to someone who's never seen it before?

Undeterred, he acted again. With the help of a colleague, he revised the proposal (presumably adding more boxes and lines), and presented it again in 1990. This time he got the go-ahead. If the story of the Web was a video game, this was unlocking a major achievement, allowing Berners-Lee to level-up. Now the *real* work began.

When Edison perfected an incandescent lightbulb for the masses, he also had to invent hundreds of other parts to make the system work, from light switches to power meters to electrical wiring. He had to develop a method of running electrical wire into the home at a reasonable price. Then he had to create machines to generate electrical power, power plants to house the ma-chines, and companies to run the power plants. The lightbulb was a tiny piece: Edison's real genius was developing the system (lighting), the meta-system (electric power), then the meta-meta-system (the electric power industry).

Similarly, Berners-Lee had to create the first web browser, the first web editor, and the first web server. The genius of Berners-Lee was that he was able to accomplish all these steps without being overwhelmed by the scale of the project. The magnitude of what he built is really astonishing—that he could see all these nonexistent pieces in his mind, and build them all, one by one.

Sir Tim, as he is now known, said that his key insight was going meta on the problem: "It was a step of generalising, going to a higher level of ab-straction, thinking about all the documentation systems out there as being possibly part of a larger imaginary documentation system."[5]

I adore this story, because it brings together so many pieces of the mind hacking program: from thinking at a higher level, to visualizing what he wanted to achieve, iterating, collaborating, and finally acting. An idea as big as the Web, in the sphere of a lesser mind, would not have gone anywhere. But Sir Tim was able to take that idea and **act**.

If you've ever been tripped up by procrastination, indecision, or just plain laziness on the way to your dreams, our final chapter will teach you skills to act. Based on the latest research, here's how to take your big ideas out of your mind and into the world.

The Power of Tiny Goals

David Blaine is the Harry Houdini of our time, an endurance artist who has performed record-breaking feats such as being encased in a block of ice for several days, buried underneath a 3-ton tank of water for a week, and sealed inside a Plexiglas case dangling over the river Thames for a month and a half. If you're looking for someone who is able to accomplish difficult long-term goals, David Blaine is your man.

To perform these feats of endurance, Blaine must be in top physical and mental condition. He eats well, reads regularly, does charity work, avoids alcohol, and is perfectly efficient with his time. Leading up to a stunt, Blaine is the model of discipline and self-control. Reportedly, he goes without food for up to a week before his stunts, to avoid soiling himself while submerged in a tank.

But in between his shows, David Blaine gets fat.

In Roy F. Baumeister and John Tierney's *Willpower: Rediscovering the Greatest Human Strength*, Blaine admits that when he's not on the clock, he kind of lets himself go. "After a stunt I'll go from 180 pounds to 230 pounds in three months," he confesses. "I waste a lot of time. I'll drink. I'll do silly things." Then, when it's time to get back in training mode, "I'll drop about three pounds a week . . . so in five months, I'm completely transformed and my discipline levels are really high."[6]

The technique that Blaine uses to get back into shape is one that any of us can use: **acting on tiny goals**. When he goes back in training, he says, "I make tons of weird goals for myself. Like, when I'm jogging in the park in the bike lane, whenever I go over a drawing of a biker, I have to step on it. And not just step on it—I have to hit the head of the biker perfectly with my foot, so that it fits right under my sneaker."

He then explains the magic formula: "*Getting your brain wired into little goals and achieving them, that helps you achieve the bigger things you shouldn't be able to do.*"

Think back to Dr. Richard Peabody, who had recovering alcoholics sit down at the end of each day and write down the next day's schedule. The power of that practice was that the alcoholic could make a list of tiny goals that could all be accomplished within twenty-four hours. Achieving those small goals creates a kind of rhythm, a positive momentum that slowly turns the alcoholic's negative spiral into a positive one.

One of the reasons so many of us fail at our goals is that we try to take it all on at once. Every year at my health club, there is a huge influx of new members on January 1. Every workout machine is filled with sweaty people gasping for air, trying to fulfill their New Year's resolutions. You can tell these folks are making the all-or-nothing kind of resolutions, such as "I will work out every day this year." Because every year, sometime around mid-January, they vanish.

In mind hacking, you've imagined some big, hairy, audacious goals for yourself. In order to accomplish those goals, you're going to have to *do the work*. You have to act. And you will be much more likely to succeed if you break down your primary goal into a series of tiny goals—as small as you need!

You don't get in shape by going to the gym every single day, starting January 1; you get in shape by going to the gym *today*. You don't stop smoking by vowing to never pick up a cigarette again; you stop for *today*. You don't earn a billion dollars overnight; you work hard at earning money *today*.

Sometimes, even the one-day-at-a-time approach is too much and you need to break it down smaller still. If you can't make it to the gym regularly, try going for a walk at lunchtime. If you can't stay on a diet, try challenging yourself to drink a large glass of water. If you're trying to complete a huge project and you're so overwhelmed that you procrastinate working on it, try working on it for fifteen minutes.

Don't get around to it,
Just get up and do it.

Finding the "tiny goals" that will help you move forward on the big goals is both an art and a science. Fortunately, there's an algorithm that will help you—or, more accurately, an *acronym*.

Focusing Your Mind Like a LASER

A laser is focused light.

Light is all around us: in the sunlight outside, the fluorescent lights overhead, the screen that you may be staring into right now. A laser takes that light and *focuses it* into a high-powered beam that can cut through steel, destroy missiles from space, or accompany the Allman Brothers. In fact, LASER was originally an acronym for "light amplification by stimulated emission of radiation." I love that acronym, because it shows a laser is essentially *amplified light.*

Similarly, the energy of our minds is usually diffused over many different thoughts, fears, memories, and time-wasting daydreams. With mind hacking, we are focusing this mental energy, much as a laser powerfully focuses light into a diamond-cutting beam of power. This focused mental energy lets us set and accomplish the tiny goals that move us toward the big goals. Just like the original LASER, there is an acronym that can help us define a good subgoal: one that is Limited, Achievable, Specific, Evaluated, and Repeatable.

- **Limited.** A good subgoal is small. Dr. Peabody asked recovering alcoholics to list every item on their schedule for the next day, including periods of rest. For the alcoholic, crossing "Take a nap" off a to-do list might seem silly, but it provides positive momentum: *I set my mind to do this small thing, then I did it.* A limited subgoal like "Work on my app for three hours this week" is better than "Add new feature X to app," since feature X may end up taking forty hours.

- **Achievable.** A good subgoal is *something you can actually accomplish.* Again, being able to point to a tiny goal that you achieved creates an upward spiral, where making progress motivates you to make more progress. "I will exercise for twenty minutes, three times this week" is a better subgoal than "Lose forty pounds by May." Small successes tend to snowball into bigger successes.

- **Specific.** A good subgoal is simple and clear. Most people have only a vague idea of what they want in life, and a vague idea of how to go about getting it. The skills you're learning in this book are teaching you to be *specific* with your mind about what you want, and now you must be *specific* about the next step in getting there. For example, "I will research online schools for half an hour today" is a better subgoal than the vague and fuzzy "Look into going back to college."

- **Evaluated.** It's important to figure out, "Did I do it?" *Write down your subgoals,* so that you can come back on a daily and weekly basis and see whether you actually accomplished them. If not, why not? Evaluating your subgoals can help you identify the issues that are holding you back ("I was too busy," "I got caught up in a TV show," "I overslept"), figure out strategies for overcoming them, and create better subgoals in the future.

- **Repeatable.** Repetition is key. While some subgoals are one-shot deals ("Enter motocross competition," "Introduce myself to world leader"), the best subgoals are the ones that you can turn into a regular habit, a flywheel of success. "I will go to one support group this week," "I will study for half an hour today," and "I will practice my concentration game this morning" are all tiny goals that will be immensely powerful if repeated over time, like a LASER.

An easy way to get started with these tiny goals is to simply ask, *What's the next step?* If you want to get free of your anxiety, what's the next step? (Practice your concentration game today.) If you want to start your own llama grooming business, what's the next step? (Spend an hour researching competitors this week.) If you want to win the Nobel Peace Prize, what's the next step? (Get rid of your semiautomatic weapons.) Then run them through the LASER test, and *act.*

You already know the laser-like power of these tiny goals, because you've been practicing them for years. When your fourth-grade teacher gave you daily multiplication drills, when your boss asks you for a weekly status report, when a social media website encourages you to "make your profile 100 percent complete," they're all leveraging the power of tiny goals. In mind hacking, we're now managing *ourselves*, setting tiny goals rather than having others set them for us.

To paraphrase former U.S. Army chief of staff Creighton Abrams, "How do you eat an elephant? *One bite at a time.*" Sir Tim Berners-Lee didn't try to swallow the entire World Wide Web; he just took the tiny bite of drafting up a proposal for his boss. Day by day, piece by piece, he built the tools needed for the Web to flourish. You can eat the elephant, too, if you focus on taking *one bite at a time.*

Psychologist Richard Wiseman created a large-scale scientific survey involving over five thousand participants trying to achieve big goals like the ones we've been discussing: losing weight, starting a business, and learning new skills. One of the key findings was that *people who broke their goal into a series of tiny goals were far more successful*—in essence, creating a step-by-step plan for getting to their goals. "These plans were especially powerful," Wiseman reports, "when the subgoals were concrete, measurable, and time-based."[7] Focused, in other words, like a LASER.

Skillfully defining these tiny goals, then acting on them, gives you a feeling of accomplishment and satisfaction. Tiny goals give you confidence to tackle bigger goals. Like a cartoon snowball rolling down a hill (I've never seen a real snowball do this, but it looks fantastic in cartoons), these little goals accumulate. Doing just a little bit builds your momentum to do more.

But there's another reason to think in terms of tiny goals: it's *fun.*

Your Life Is a Video Game

One of my favorite video games is called *Beautiful Katamari*, which is one of those fantastically insane creations that could only come from Japan. In the game, you start with a tiny sphere, a kind of sticky snowball called a *katamari*. Using your controller, you roll this sphere through different environments— a candy shop or a fast-food restaurant—rolling over random objects like poker chips and wheels of cheese, gradually making your *katamari* bigger.

As the game progresses, your *katamari* gets big enough to roll through towns, picking up farm animals and boats. It's wildly hilarious to see struggling cows and people hanging on to the side of your *katamari* as it gathers mass. Then you move to the city level, picking up buildings and amusement park rides. Eventually your *katamari* is big enough to roll over landmasses on the face of the earth, until finally you're in space, picking up planets and stars.

There's an odd kind of satisfaction at each tiny accumulation in *Beautiful Katamari*, because our minds—especially geek minds—are wired to accumulate. This is something video game designers have known since the earliest days: the point system of *Space Invaders* begat the level system of *Pac-Man*, which begat the world system of *Super Mario Bros.*, which begat the current systems of badges, leaderboards, hidden levels, unlockable weapons, and Easter eggs. There are even meta-scoring systems like Xbox's "Gamerscore," which accumulates achievements across every Xbox game you've played.

All these systems are based on tiny subgoals: complete this mission, finish this level, make it through this challenge. As we discussed at the beginning of this book, the geek mind loves to control and possess a small portion of the world, to know everything there is to know. It drives my kids crazy when we're playing a video game together and I have to find every hidden treasure, unlocking 100 percent of the characters and costumes. But this is the fun of video games: mastering tiny goals that give us tiny rewards, until one day we've conquered the game.

When we think of our personal subgoals like the missions in video games, we can shift our mind-set from "work" to "fun." After all, video games *are* a kind of work: you have to learn new skills, think through problems, and compete hard against other players. But somehow it doesn't *feel* like work, because there are tangible rewards along the way: you can see how far you've come.

Whatever your geek passion, whether it's collecting comics, learning LARPing, or studying stars, there's a feeling of accumulation, a feeling of mastery. Putting your tiny goals into this same mental model—whether it's earning points or collecting power-ups or completing 100 percent of your missions—is one of the best mind hacks I can recommend. Seeing your tiny goals as a geeky challenge keeps you motivated.

Game designer Jane McGonigal sees *life itself* as a kind of video game. In her famous TED talk titled "The Game That Can Add 10 Years to Your Life," McGonigal shared how she used game thinking to heal herself from a debilitating head injury. After receiving a concussion that left her suffering from nausea, headaches, and mental fog, the advice from her doctor was just to let her brain rest: no reading, writing, or video games. "In other words," she jokes, "no reason to live."[8]

She did, in fact, begin to suffer from suicidal thoughts, which is common with traumatic brain injuries. The thoughts began to grow so pervasive and intense that they finally led her to a life-changing moment. "I am either going to kill myself," she vowed, "or I'm going to turn this into a game."

She created a mental game for herself called Jane the Concussion Slayer. This was a mind hack where she awarded herself points for avoiding "bad guys" that triggered her symptoms (bright lights, crowded spaces) and more points for collecting power-ups that helped her heal (getting out of bed, taking a walk). Within a couple of days, she reports, the fog of depression and anxiety went away. While the cognitive symptoms and headaches took another year to heal, the game gave her the power to focus on tiny goals that eventually helped her achieve the big goals.

This experience was the basis of not only McGonigal's TED talk but also her *New York Times* best-selling book, *Reality Is Broken: Why Games Make Us Better and How They Can Change the World.* In it, she argues that many of the world's greatest problems, from childhood obesity to global warming, can be solved by approaching them as video games: making tiny goals and achievements that, over time, can lead to epic wins.

Throughout *Mind Hacking*, we've been presenting our exercises as Mind Games, because there *is* a gamelike component to mastering the mind: we must develop unfamiliar skills in a virtual world, working toward long-term goals while focusing on beating the current level. Now, as we move out of our mind and into the world, you can assign points to setting and achieving specific subgoals, which keeps you motivated until you finally conquer the boss level and look with satisfaction at the end credits.

MIND GAME

The LASER

Each day, after your concentration game, write down your positive loops, then spend sixty seconds in mental simulation on one goal. Then write down one LASER-focused subgoal that will move you toward that goal, asking yourself, "What's the next baby step?"

Write down and check off each subgoal on your practice sheet.

Pushing the Swing

Think about pushing a child on a swing set. If you want to get the kid swinging higher, when do you push?

You get the most swing for your push if you do it at *the beginning of the upswing*—just as the child comes back and starts heading in the other direction. If you try pushing while the child is flying back toward you, your energy is wasted: you will actually *slow down the swing*, and possibly break your finger.

Now, that's a weird concept. It's the same amount of force but, applied at one time on the swing cycle, it pushes the child higher, and at another time it slows the kid down. The swing, which is a pendulum, has a natural interval, a kind of beat or tempo. Pushing the swing in time with this tempo will cause it to go higher. In other words, *small pushes, when timed correctly, can have big effects.*

In physics, this is called **resonance**, the natural tendency of objects to vibrate in sync with some external force. This concept is to be found throughout nature. Objects like organ pipes, quartz crystals, and, yes, LASER rods operate on the principle of resonance. Pluck the string on an acoustic guitar, and you're hearing the sympathetic vibrations of the finely crafted guitar body, which is why it sounds so much more beautiful than a rubber band stretched across a cardboard box.

Acoustic resonance is how you can shatter a crystal wineglass with sound played at the right resonant frequency: the glass molecules will vibrate in sync with the sound waves until eventually the glass breaks apart. There is also *tidal resonance*, such as in the Bay of Fundy off Maine, where the continental shelf is a width that amplifies the natural resonance of the ocean, causing the highest tidal range in the world. There is *orbital resonance*, where two orbiting bodies exert a regular gravitational pull on each other, such as that found between Earth and Venus.

Resonance is so pervasive that Nikola Tesla once wrote, "If you want to find the secrets of the universe, think in terms of energy, frequency and vibration." Which brings us back to our concept of tiny repeatable goals: when timed correctly, they can have big effects.

I've always been a hard worker, even back in the days when I smoked a lot of marijuana. I was not the stereotypical stoner watching cartoons while eating Twinkies filled with Cheez Whiz. First, the Twinkies were usually filled with Nutella. Also, the weed gave me a kind of creative inspiration, the constant *aha!* moments that fueled me to be even more creative. So I would always be working, following whatever ridiculous ideas my pot-soaked brain would dream up.

While this occasionally produced some genuine inspiration, I see now that there was a lack of coherence to my efforts: one day I would be excited about creating a new social media project, the next day a T-shirt line. Most bakeheads are unable to see *any* projects through to completion, so I figured those rules didn't apply to me, because I was able to get so much stuff done.

However, getting stuff done is not nearly as important as getting the *right* stuff done. Much of the time I was pushing *against* the swing, pushing the kid *out of* the swing, or running underneath the child and getting *bludgeoned* by the swing. I was bewildered by how I could be working so hard and yet making so little progress. One of the tremendous gifts that sobriety gave me was the *clarity* to see the tiny goals that could have the biggest impact on my overall goals—and this plays out in every area of my life.

It started with the daily goal of staying sober. Before sobriety, I spent an incredible amount of time thinking about how and when I was going to get high. I didn't want anyone to notice it, so I had to plan my day around finding a convenient place, getting rid of the smell, trying to act normally afterward—a cycle that would often be repeated *several times a day*. This consumed a ridiculous amount of mental energy.

The small, repeatable goal of *staying sober* freed up all that mental energy. It was like I had been swimming with a cinder block chained to my waist, and I was able to remove the padlock and let the cinder block drop free. I was then able to focus all that newfound energy back on my own negative loops, gradually untangling the knots of buggy code, then reprogramming my mind to achieve more positive and constructive goals.

Each day I practiced my concentration exercises, each time I repeated my positive loops, I was pushing the swing a little higher. Like a pendulum, I found the system gives you energy back, swinging you higher and higher. I began making goals for the real world, expanding my business, my network, my vision of what we can achieve together. Once you find the natural cycle, you can gradually add energy to increase those cycles.

With this book, with this crowdsourced system of mind hacking, my hope is that *you* can begin pushing your own swing higher and higher. And not just you but thousands and millions of mind hackers worldwide. I can think of no higher swing than all of us learning how to harness the human mind together.

Increasing Your Willpower

Let's say you make a tiny goal of walking for five minutes a day. No *I'm going to the gym every day until I can fit in a size 1 dress*, just *I'm going to park my car at the far end of the parking lot at work*. And because this is a LASER goal, you can actually achieve it.

After a few weeks of accomplishing your goal, you're feeling pretty good. You find yourself saying, *Hey, I'm already walking; may as well walk around the parking lot once more before I go home.* You tell a friend about your little experiment, and the two of you start doing it together.

Then you find yourself thinking about how to log your walks. You spend the money for an exercise tracker, and now you and your friend start sharing data with each other. Maybe you start setting daily goals and sharing them via social network.

Now you're taking longer walks over lunch, and soon you're finding that you have more energy and you're less winded than when you started. You realize you'd be even *less* winded if you stopped smoking, so you buy a box of nicotine patches and start drinking a lot of water instead.

After a few weeks, you have even *more* energy, so you take the money you were spending on cigarettes and buy a cheap gym membership. You and your friend now meet before work, and you find that the early-morning workout actually helps you get more accomplished on the job.

After another few months of this, your boss dies of a meat-related heart attack and, noticing the amazing job you have done, senior management promotes you to his position at a 21 percent raise. Now you're not only feeling better, you're making more money and you have more power.

You begin to see ways of improving your small team, so you begin implementing some of the methods of mind hacking that you've learned here. After six months, your team is transformed into the highest-performing team in the company, and senior management begins to take notice.

At this point, you realize there is an amazing opportunity in this market that your company does not see. You quit your job and create an app that quickly grows to one hundred million users. Within a year, a Chinese tech company offers to buy your app for one hundred million dollars, or a dollar per user.

With that money, you join a group of investors trying to create a crowd-sourced solution for worldwide peace. Recruiting the world's thousand richest people, the group pools together trillions of dollars, eventually overcoming the world's war budget and establishing planetary happiness.

So you see, the five-minute walk was time well spent.

This is what author Charles Duhigg calls a "keystone habit." Often, creating one positive habit—always through a series of LASER-like goals—will start a domino effect with other positive changes. You often see this happen with recovering alcoholics: within a year, they've not only stopped drinking but quit smoking and lost weight, and are having the best sex of their lives. It doesn't always happen this way, but it happens often enough to notice: one positive change can have cascading effects through your life.

In *Willpower*, Baumeister and Tierney point to new research studies showing that willpower is a kind of energy, a battery that can be recharged. They outline various methods of *increasing* willpower, such as exercise, sleep, and concentration, which in turn increase your power to act. Similarly, the Mind Games throughout this book are designed to increase your mental energy, which will increase your willpower, which will increase your ability to make meaningful change in the world.

The swing goes higher and higher.

The Final Frontier

Here's a final question to ponder: *Who are you?*

We started out by establishing that you are not your mind. But if "you" are not your mind, then who—or *what*—is the "you"?

Thinking deeply about this question will reveal a weird recursive loop. If "I" am watching "me," then who is the "I" who's watching *that*? It seems to echo back into infinity, like:

- The long tunnel of reflections when you stand between two mirrors

- The "infinite video loop" that occurs when you point a video camera at a monitor displaying the live feed

- Audio feedback, which is sound from the speaker being amplified by the microphone in a self-reinforcing loop

- Recursive acronyms (like Richard Stallman's GNU, which stands for GNU's Not Unix, but then *what does GNU stand for?*)

- Fractals, which are made of patterns that repeat themselves at any scale

- Much of the work of M. C. Escher, such as the two hands drawing each other

- The Department of Redundancy Department

- Which came first: the chicken or the egg?

Who are you? You're the one viewing "you." But then who are *you?*

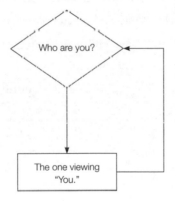

Here is where we enter the realm of the philosopher and the mystic. But I want to encourage a more scientific, *exploratory* approach to this question. Embrace the question like a geek. After all, *recursion* (bits of code that can call themselves) is a central idea of programming: to calculate factorials, for example, we create a function that can continually call itself, until all the factorials have been determined. "To understand recursion," as the geek joke goes, "one must first understand recursion."

Finding the real "you" shows you the limits of our current models. There is no satisfying logical answer to the question, because the "you" seems to always jump one step outside your objective mind. Even if you're a crazy-smart logic genius who can hold six levels of recursion in your head, you're still an infinity away from solving the problem.

Finding the *you* behind "you" is the ultimate mystery. *Star Trek* was wrong: space is not the final frontier. *This* is the final frontier, this exploration beyond the mind. We've been calling this infinite frontier "you," but that's as far as words can take us. We cannot put a name on it, because to name it is to bring it back into the realm of the mind. If we try to describe its attributes, we are only pulling away pieces of it, like taffy. *What is behind the mind?*

This is what we have been leading up to, what all this work is about. As you learn to get your mind out of the way, to control it rather than being controlled by it, something else opens up. The "you" that's now controlling the mind—that mysterious frontier—is ultimately what we're after. Throughout this book are scattered clues that explain the nature of this frontier. They are hidden in every chapter. If you search for them diligently, you will find them. It is, I believe, life's most satisfying search.

And now, faithful mind hacker, we come to our final loop.

```
}
$numreads++;
if ($numreads == 1){
    ReadBook();
} else {
    JoinCommunity();
    ImproveProgram();
    ChangeWorld();
}

# It's my sincere hope that the technology of
mind hacking will help you change your mind.
For good.
```

\<PRACTICE SHEET>

Mind hacking is a *skill*, but it's also a *system*. This practice sheet is designed to embed this system into your life and mind using easy daily goals. Have fun with it! Approach the Mind Games with a spirit of playfulness, like a mental video game. You'll find that mastering them is both powerful and satisfying, like learning to wield a light saber.

Getting started on Day 1 is the hardest part; once you've conquered that goal, you will level-up as you hit certain progress milestones. Keep your energy focused on today's small goal, and don't worry if you miss a day here or there—hop right back into the program. Hack hard and prosper.

Get the app! It's a free download at:
www.mindhacki.ng

Day 1: Accepting the Quest

Write "Hello, World!" Then decide on a *specific* time and place you will practice mind hacking each day, and keep the book in that spot as a visual reminder.

Date	"Hello, World!"	Daily practice time	Daily practice location

Day 2: What Was My Mind Just Thinking?

Start building up awareness of your mind by asking yourself, as frequently as possible, "What was my mind just thinking?" Keep track of how many times you remember to "check in" on your mind today.

Date	Awareness Points	Observations

Day 3: Squirrel!

For the rest of the day, try to become aware of whenever your attention is pulled away from the task at hand by either digital or human interruptions. Try to become aware of the feeling of "broken flow" when you lose your concentration. Keep track of how many interruptions you notice, and write down your total score.

Date	Positive	Negative	Awareness Points
Observations			

Day 4: The One-Hour Investment

Spend one hour cleaning out or turning off unnecessary digital distractions, including instant messaging, text messaging, notifications and alerts, time-wasting Internet sites, and unnecessary emails. Count the number of digital distractions you turned off, and record that number below.

BONUS: Check off the bonus box if you set a recurring appointment in your calendar to review and eliminate further once a month.

Date	Awareness Points	Bonus

Day 5: The Concentration Game

Today is a big day: the first day of your concentration training. Put on the helmet, grab your light saber, and let's begin.

- Choose a consistent time and place to practice your concentration game. (Morning is best, before the daily routine kicks in.)

- Decide on a *consistent* reward when you're finished (smoothie, shower, sleep).

- Find a comfortable place to sit, reasonably quiet and free from distractions.

- Sit with your legs crossed, or feet on the ground. If you find yourself getting drowsy, stand.

- Close your eyes and focus on your breath.

- Relax each part of your body, starting from the top of your head, your forehead, eyes, cheeks, mouth, jaw, etc., down through your toes, then back up again. This process should take 2 to 3 minutes.

- Mentally tell your mind what you are going to do, e.g., *For the next twenty minutes, I will focus on the breath, so that I may develop superhuman concentration.*

- Now focus on the breath at the fleshy part where your nostrils meet.

- When you find yourself following your mind ("lost in the movie"), simply redirect it back to the breath at the nostrils. Score +1 point for noticing, and calmly redirect back to your breath.

- Keep track of your points on your fingers, or in your head.

- You can set a soft timer or alarm for twenty minutes; eventually you'll develop a feel for when twenty minutes have passed.

Record your final score, and check off the reward box as a reward for your reward.

Date	Awareness Points	Reward
Observations		

LEVEL UP! Research shows that you are far more likely to succeed if you record your progress for five successive days. Congratulations!

Day 6: The Concentration Game

Follow the instructions from the previous day until they become second nature. Be sure to reinforce yourself with your post-concentration reward, and check off the box. Keep the reward consistent.

Date	Awareness Points	Reward
Observations		

Day 7: The Concentration Game + Name That Loop

Today, in addition to your concentration game, spend the day trying to "catch" your negative mind loops as they happen. Watch for signs of mental "pain" or friction, which are a good indicator of thought processes that need debugging.

Debug each negative thought loop down to its bare METAL (My Emotion-Thought-Action Loop), using one of the three techniques:

- **The Five Whys:** Ask *Why?* five times.

- **Worst-Case Scenario:** What's the worst thing that could happen?

- **Third-Person Perspective:** What would you say if you were hearing this from someone else?

Date	Awareness Points	Reward
Observations		

Emotion	Thought(s)	Action(s)

Day 8: The Concentration Game + Name That Loop

Follow the previous day's instructions. Be sure to treat yourself to the reward.

Date	Awareness Points	Reward
Observations		

Root problem	METAL

Day 9: The Concentration Game + Name That Loop

Once more, follow the previous day's instructions. Don't forget the reward!

Date	Awareness Points	Reward
Observations		

Root problem	METAL

Day 10: The Concentration Game + The Five Words

Today, play your concentration game as usual. Then complete the five imagination games in Section 2.2. Write down one word for each. (It's better to get it done than get it perfect: you can always add more later.)

- **Feel:** The Mood Chip

- **Do:** The $50 Million Inheritance

- **Have:** The Genie in the Lamp

- **Give:** Your Evolution Contribution

- **Be:** The Funeral Speech

Date	Awareness Points	Reward
Observations		

Game	Your Word
Feel	
Do	
Have	
Give	
Be	

Day 11: The Concentration Game + Write Now

After completing your daily concentration game, write down each of your positive loops in your notebook or digital device.

Date	Awareness Points	Reward
Observations		

Positive Goal	Positive Loop
Feel	
Do	
Have	
Give	
Be	

Day 12: The Concentration Game + Write Now

Follow the previous day's instructions, and lock it in with a reward.

Date	Awareness Points	Reward
Observations			

Positive Goal	Positive Loop
Feel	
Do	
Have	
Give	
Be	

Day 13: The Concentration Game + Write Now

A great day to reread the instructions for the concentration game. Don't forget the reward!

Date	Awareness Points	Reward
Observations			

Positive Goal	Positive Loop
Feel	
Do	
Have	
Give	
Be	

Day 14: The Concentration Game + Write Now

The concentration game, followed by the written exercise, followed by a reward.

Date	Awareness Points	Reward
Observations		

Positive Goal	Positive Loop
Feel	
Do	
Have	
Give	
Be	

Day 15: The Concentration Game +
Write Now + Reminding Your Mind

Today, do the concentration game, followed by the written exercise, followed by a reward. Then set up a reminder system for yourself, similar to the ideas in Section 3.2, that will repeatedly bring one of your positive loops to mind:

- **Repetition Reminders:** The $10 Million Check

- **Repetition Trackers:** Don't Break the Chain

- **Talking to Yourself:** Smiling in the Shower

Date	Awareness Points	Reward
Observations		

Positive Goal	Positive Loop
Feel	
Do	
Have	
Give	
Be	

Reminder system

Day 16: The Concentration Game + Write Now + The Simulator

After completing your daily concentration game and writing down your positive loops, spend sixty seconds doing a mental simulation on one of these loops, using one of the techniques mentioned here:

- **Shall We Play a Game?:** simulating the steps involved with getting to your goal

- **Block and Tackle:** simulating specific difficulties and how you will overcome them

- **Self-Simulation:** seeing yourself in the third person

Score a bonus for completing the one-minute simulation.

Date	Awareness Points	Simulator Bonus	Reward
Observations			

Positive Goal	Positive Loop
Feel	
Do	
Have	
Give	
Be	

Day 17: The Concentration Game + Write Now + The Simulator

Do the concentration game, the written exercise, one of the simulation exercises, then a consistent reward. The entire process should take less than half an hour.

Date	Awareness Points	Simulator Bonus	Reward
Observations			

Positive Goal	Positive Loop
Feel	
Do	
Have	
Give	
Be	

Day 18: The Concentration Game + Write Now + The Simulator

The concentration game, the written exercise, one of the simulation exercises, and your reward.

Date	Awareness Points	Simulator Bonus	Reward
Observations			

Positive Goal	Positive Loop
Feel	
Do	
Have	
Give	
Be	

Day 19: The Concentration Game + Write Now + The Simulator + Share the Dream

Follow your concentration/writing/simulation process as usual. Today, also share one of your positive loops with someone else: a friend, relative, or other trusted confidant. Be brave! Research shows that sharing your goals with someone else makes you more likely to achieve them.

Date	Awareness Points	Simulator Bonus	Reward
Observations			

Positive Goal	Positive Loop
Feel	
Do	
Have	
Give	
Be	

Name of confidant

Day 20: The Concentration Game + Write Now
+ The Simulator + The LASER

After your concentration/writing/simulation process, you should now write down **one** small subgoal that will move you toward **one** of your simulated goals, asking yourself, *What's the next baby step to achieve this goal?* Use the LASER criteria, and write down this subgoal.

Date	Awareness Points	Simulator Bonus	Reward
Observations			

Positive Goal	Positive Loop	LASER Subgoal (one)
Feel		
Do		
Have		
Give		
Be		

Day 21: The Concentration Game + Write Now + The Simulator + The LASER

Repeat instructions from the previous day, crossing off yesterday's LASER subgoal if you've accomplished it. If not, consider making your subgoal even simpler (something you can accomplish today), or moving to a different goal.

Date	Awareness Points	Simulator Bonus	Reward
Observations			

Positive Goal	Positive Loop	LASER Subgoal (one)
Feel		
Do		
Have		
Give		
Be		

Congratulations! You have developed a process for mind hacking that you can use for the rest of your life. You have learned to **analyze** your mind through concentration games, **imagine** new possibilities through writing and simulating, and **reprogram** your mind—and your life—through finding and acting on the next step.

Continue on with these fundamental exercises from Day 21: concentrating, writing, simulating, and acting. With this 21-Day Plan, you've made it through the first stage; from here on out, life itself provides the challenges. May you conquer the boss level with ease, and have the satisfaction of watching the end credits roll.

LEVEL UP!

Quick Reference Guide

Awareness

- **Mind Movie.** Being aware that "you" are watching a "movie" called your mind.

- **Superuser.** Imagining logging in to a more powerful account that lets you access and control your mind.

- **Metathinking.** Thinking about your thinking.

Concentration

- **Awareness Points.** A small internal reward for becoming aware of your mind. Awareness points can be used in concentration exercises, and to build mindfulness in everyday tasks.

- **Squirrel!** Becoming aware of distractions, especially digital distractions, that break your concentration (text messages, chat requests, etc.).

- **Mental Decluttering.** Reducing the "mental clutter" of unfinished tasks by eliminating interruptions.

- **Concentration Game.** Progressively relax the body, then focus on the breath at the nostrils. Score +1 Awareness Point when you notice your mind wandering.

- **The Illuminati.** Instead of focusing on the nostrils, focus on the point between the eyebrows.

- **Alien Blaster.** Pretend each thought is an alien. Whenever you notice a thought, mentally say, "Thought," which disintegrates the alien with a hydrogen-ion particle blaster.

- **The Third Nipple.** Instead of focusing on the nostrils, focus on the point between the breasts.

- **Golden Breath.** Instead of focusing on the nostrils, focus on the air itself as you inhale and exhale. Imagine that you are taking in pure oxygen, a delicious smell, or a healing elixir.

- **The Slow Jam.** Do the basic concentration game, but as you exhale, try to capture the "feel" of sinking into a warm bubble bath, relaxing into a sexy rhythm, or grooving to a slow jam.

- **Rise and Smile.** Perform any of the variations above, but smile while doing so.

Debugging

- **Five Whys.** Asking "Why?" five times, until you get to the root (or roots) of your problem thinking.

- **Worst-Case Scenario.** Asking, "What's the worst thing that could possibly happen?"

- **Third-Person Perspective.** Asking, "If this was someone else's problem, what would I say to that person?"

- **Invisible Counselors.** Imagining great historical figures who can offer advice on your problem.

- **METAL.** My Emotion-Thought-Action Loop, or identifying the emotion that precedes the thought that precedes the action.

Imagination

- **Relooping.** Taking a METAL loop and imagining a new loop to replace the old one.

- **Reality Distortion Field.** Imagining that reality has already been changed ("Fake it till you make it").

- **Your Best Possible Future.** Imagining what you want out of life (not what you *don't* want).

Positive Loops

- **The Mood Chip.** If you could have an emotional bio-chip implanted into your head, what emotion would you choose?

- **The $50 Million Inheritance.** If you suddenly inherited a large sum, what experience would you buy?

- **The Genie in the Lamp.** If you outstmarted a genie, what would you ask for?

- **Your Evolution Contribution.** What's the one thing you'd like to contribute to the world?

- **The Funeral Speech.** What's the one thing you'd like people to say about you when you die?

Repetition

- **The $10 Million Check.** Writing your positive loops somewhere you will see them regularly.

- **Don't Break the Chain.** Keeping—and recording—a daily "streak" of some positive habit.

- **Smiling in the Shower.** Repeating your positive loops during downtime, while smiling or feeling good.

Simulation

- **Shall We Play a Game?** Imagining the step-by-step *process* of getting to your goal (not just the end state).

- **Block and Tackle.** Imagining how you will respond in moments of difficulty, on your way to achieving your goal.

- **Self-Simulation.** Seeing yourself achieving your goal, but in the third person.

Collaboration

- **Share the Dream.** Sharing your positive loops and goals with other people.

Acting

- **LASER.** Choosing subgoals that are Limited, Achievable, Specific, Evaluated, and Repeatable.

Acknowledgments

End Credits

Super Agent
Cathy Hemming

Super Editor
Jeremie Ruby-Strauss

Super Publisher
Jen Bergstrom

Super Family
Jade Hargrave
Isaac Hargrave
Luke Hargrave
John Hargrave
Pat Hargrave
Patrick Hargrave
Keri Hargrave
Marguerite Thomason
Patty Vonick

Super Friends
Bob Carmichael
Jay Cornelius
Jean Egan
Chris Georgenes
Jodi Heights

Mike Hoban
Heather Kelly
Genevieve Martineau
Christy Ramsey
Joan Roman
Derek Sandstrom
Sheri Sandstrom
Jay Stevens

Promotional Coordinator
Fiona Merullo

Statistical Analyst
Kerstin Allen

Gamification Consultant
Evan Karnoupakis

Secret Advisor
Joe Vitale

Super Producers
Akasha Archer
Nina Cordes
Robert Ettlin
Nancy Tonik

Beta Readers

Tom Alan
Beth Buelow
Brian Carter
Jim Collison
J. V. Crum III
Dave Cuda
Vicki Davis
Giovanni Dienstmann
Kallen Diggs
Antonia Dodge
Roger Dooley
John Lee Dumas
Nathan Earl
Andrew Ferebee
Jason Gauci
Emily Harkins
Ryan Hawk
Vlad Ionescu
Septembre Lewis
Corbin Links
David Long
Henry Manampiring
Martin McGovern
Phil McKinney
Daudi Mugabi
Rajiv Nathan
Jake Nawrocki
Michael Neeley

Thom Obarski
Ben Orenstein
Prescott Perez-Fox
Wendy Reese
Caleb Richards
Joshua Rivers
Jena Rodriguez
Jim Simcoe
Jeff Smith
John Sonmez
Robyn Stratton-Berkessel
Brett Terpstra
Mike Vardy
Justin Verrengia
Mary Warner
John Watson
John Weldon
Patrick Wheeler
Joel Mark Witt

Quality Support

Scott Adams
Susan Blackmore
Allen Downey
Shel Kaphan
Samy Pesse
Richard Stallman
Brad Stone

Thank you to the thousands of readers and beta testers who have provided valuable feedback and continue to make mind hacking better for all of us. Join our mailing list at: www.mindhacki.ng.

Notes

What Is Mind Hacking?

1. "The Hacker's Dictionary, Version 4.3.0," Dourish.com, April 30, 2001, http://www.dourish.com/goodies/jargon.html.

2. Walter Isaacson, *Steve Jobs* (New York: Simon & Schuster, 2011), 61.

3. Ibid., 59.

4. Sam Williams, *Free as in Freedom: Richard Stallman's Crusade for Free Software* (Sebastopol, CA: O'Reilly Media, 2002), http://oreilly.com/openbook/freedom/ch01.html.

5. Ibid.

6. Richard Stallman, "Free Software Is Even More Important Now," GNU.org, http://gnu.org/philosophy/free-software-even-more-important.html.

7. "Usage statistics and market share of Unix for websites," *W3Techs*, http://w3techs.com/technologies/details/os-unix/all/all.

8. "September 2012 Web Server Survey," *Netcraft*, http://news.netcraft.com/archives/2012/09/10/september-2012-web-server-survey.html.

9. "Browser Statistics," *W3Schools*, http://www.w3schools.com/browsers/browsers_stats.asp.

10. The online version of *Mind Hacking* is licensed under a Creative Commons Attribution NonCommercial-ShareAlike 4.0 International License. For more information, see http://creativecommons.org/licenses/by-nc-sa/4.0.

11. Tim Ferriss, *The 4-Hour Body: An Uncommon Guide to Rapid Fat-Loss, Incredible Sex, and Becoming Superhuman* (New York: Crown Publishing Group, 2010), 484–89.

12. Daniel Pink, *Drive: The Surprising Truth About What Motivates Us* (New York: Riverhead Hardcover, 2009).

13. Chris Hardwick, *The Nerdist Way: How to Reach the Next Level (in Real Life)* (New York: Penguin, 2011).

14. Steven Leckart, "The Hackathon Is On: Pitching and Programming the Next Killer App," *Wired*, March 2012.

15. Stephen Lepore and Joshua Smyth, "The Writing Cure: How Expressive Writing Promotes Health and Emotional Well-Being" (Washington, DC: American Psychological Association, 2002).

16. S. Spera, E. Buhrfeind, and J. W. Pennebaker, "Expressive Writing and Coping with Job Loss," *Academy of Management Journal* 37, No. 3 (1994): 722–33. Thanks to Richard Wiseman's *59 Seconds: Change Your Life in Under a Minute* (New York: Anchor, 2010) for the finding.

1.1 You Are Not Your Mind

1. Amy Shira Teitel, "The Cost of Curiosity," AmyShiraTeitel.com, Sept. 28, 2012, http://amyshirateitel.com/2012/09/28/the-cost-of-curiosity.

2. Joe Palca, "Crazy Smart: When a Rocker Designs a Mars Lander," NPR, Aug. 3, 2012, http://www.npr.org/2012/08/03/157597270/crazy-smart -when-a-rocker-designs-a-mars-lander.

3. "Curiosity's Seven Minutes of Terror," jpl.NASA.gov, June 22, 2012, http://www.jpl.nasa.gov/video/details.php?id=1090.

4. Guy Webster and Dwayne Browne, "NASA's Mars Curiosity Rover Marks First Martian Year," NASA.gov, June 23, 2014, http://www.nasa .gov/press/2014/june/nasa-s-mars-curiosity-rover-marks-first-martian -year-with-mission-successes.

5. "Mars Science Laboratory: Mission Science Goals," NASA.gov, Aug. 21, 2012, http://mars.nasa.gov/msl/mission/science/goals.

6. Susan Blackmore, *Consciousness: An Introduction* (London: Routledge, 2010). Blackmore literally wrote the book on consciousness, and her exercises are the inspiration for the Mind Games in this book. The purpose of Blackmore's exercises is to show you the illusory nature of the mind, and I highly recommend her book for advanced mind hackers.

7. Sylvia Nasar, "The sum of a man," *Guardian*, March 25, 2002, http://www.theguardian.com/books/2002/mar/26/biography.highereducation.

8. Tore Frängsmyr (ed.), *Les Prix Nobel: The Nobel Prizes 1994* (Stockholm: Nobel Foundation, 1994), http://www.nobelprize.org/nobel_prizes/economic-sciences/laureates/1994/nash-bio.html.

9. "Glimpsing Inside a Beautiful Mind," Schizophrenia.com, April 10, 2005, http://www.schizophrenia.com/sznews/archives/001617.html.

10. Sylvia Nasar, *A Beautiful Mind: A Biography of John Forbes Nash, Jr., Winner of the Nobel Prize in Economics, 1994* (New York: Simon & Schuster, 1998).

11. John Milnor, "John Nash and the Beautiful Mind," *Notices of the American Mathematical Society* 45, No. 10 (1998): 1329.

12. Wendy Hasenkamp and Lawrence W. Barsalou, "Effects of Meditation Experience on Functional Connectivity of Distributed Brain Networks," *Frontiers in Human Neuroscience*, March 1, 2012.

13. Daniel Goleman, "Exercising the Mind to Treat Attention Deficits," *New York Times*, May 12, 2014, http://well.blogs.nytimes.com/2014/05/12/exercising-the-mind-to-treat-attention-deficits.

14. See Douglas Hofstadter's excellent book *I Am a Strange Loop* (New York: Basic Books, 2007) for a fascinating explanation of the mind-bending work of mathematician Kurt Gödel.

1.2 Your Mind Has a Mind of Its Own

1. Thomas H. Davenport and John C. Beck, *The Attention Economy: Understanding the New Currency of Business* (Boston: Harvard Business School Press, 2002).

2. Robert Rogers and Stephen Monsell, "The Costs of a Predictable Switch Between Simple Cognitive Tasks," *Journal of Experimental Psychology: General* 124, No. 2 (1995): 207–31.

3. Joshua S. Rubinstein, David E. Meyer, and Jeffrey E. Evans, "Executive Control of Cognitive Processes in Task Switching," *Journal of Experi-*

mental Psychology: Human Perception and Performance 27, No. 4 (2001): 763–97.

4. Edward M. Hallowell, *Crazy Busy: Overstretched, Overbooked, and About to Snap! Strategies for Handling Your Fast-Paced Life* (New York: Ballantine Books, 2007).

5. Bill Chappell, "Stanford Professor Who Sounded Alert on Multitasking Has Died," *NPR*, Nov. 7, 2013, http://www.npr.org/blogs/thetwo -way/2013/11/07/243762058/stanford-professor-who-sounded-alert -on-multitasking-has-died (accessed Dec. 1, 2013). Emphasis mine.

6. Soren Gordhamer, *Wisdom 2.0: Ancient Secrets for the Creative and Constantly Connected* (New York: HarperOne, 2009).

7. "ADHD Data and Statistics," *Centers for Disease Control and Prevention*, Nov. 13, 2013, http://www.cdc.gov/ncbddd/adhd/data.html.

8. "Frequent Cell Phone Use Linked to Anxiety, Lower Grades and Reduced Happiness in Students, Kent State Research Shows," Kent State University, Dec. 6, 2013, http://www2.kent.edu/news/news-detail.cfm ?newsitem=C87DA8EB-0E77-DCF2-AAD1C317FB742933.

9. "Turn Off Your Smart Phone to Beat Stress," *British Psychological Society*, Dec. 1, 2012, http://www.bps.org.uk/news/turn-your-smart-phone -beat-stress.

1.3 Developing Jedi-Like Concentration

1. William James, *The Principles of Psychology* (New York: H. Holt and Company, 1890), chapter 11.

2. H. Pashler, J. Johnston, and E. Ruthruff, "Attention and Performance," *Annual Review of Psychology* 52, No. 1 (2001): 629–51.

3. Benedict Carey, "Remembering, as an Extreme Sport," *New York Times*, May 19, 2014, http://well.blogs.nytimes.com/2014/05/19/remember ing-as-an-extreme-sport.

4. Tim Wu, "How Today's Computers Weaken Our Brain," *New Yorker*, Sept. 9, 2013, http://www.newyorker.com/tech/elements/how-todays -computers-weaken-our-brain.

5. B. V. Zeigarnik, "Über das Behalten von erledigten und unerledigten Handlungen" ("The retention of completed and uncompleted activities"), *Psychologische Forschung*, No. 9 (1927): 1–85.

6. Walter Isaacson, *Steve Jobs*, 39.

7. Amishi P. Jha, Jason Krompinger, and Michael J. Baime, "Mindfulness Training Modifies Subsystems of Attention," *Cognitive, Affective, & Behavioral Neuroscience* 7, No. 2 (2007): 109–119.

8. Antoine Lutz, Heleen A. Slagter, John D. Dunne, and Richard J. Davidson, "Attention Regulation and Monitoring in Meditation," *Trends in Cognitive Sciences* 12, No. 4 (2008): 163–69.

9. Richard J. Davidson, Jon Kabat-Zinn, Jessica Schumacher, Melissa Rosenkranz, Daniel Muller, Saki F. Santorelli, Ferris Urbanowski, Anne Harrington, Katherine Bonus, and John F. Sheridan, "Alterations in Brain and Immune Function Produced by Mindfulness Meditation," *Psychosomatic Medicine* 65, No. 4 (2003). 564–70.

10. Sean Barnes, Kirk Warren Brown, Elizabeth Krusemark, W. Keith Campbell, and Ronald D. Rogge, "The Role of Mindfulness in Romantic Relationship Satisfaction and Reponses to Relationship Stress," *Journal of Marital and Family Therapy* 33, No. 4 (Oct. 2007): 482–500.

11. Richard J. Davidson et al., "Alterations in Brain and Immune Function Produced by Mindfulness Meditation," *Psychosomatic Medicine* 65, No. 4 (July 2003): 564–70.

12. Charles Duhigg, *The Power of Habit: Why We Do What We Do in Life and Business* (New York: Random House, 2012).

13. Daniel Ingram, *Mastering the Core Teachings of the Buddha* (London: Aeon Books, 2008). I am indebted to Ingram for many of the concentration variations in this chapter. I highly recommend his book as a technical manual for those looking to master higher levels of concentration.

1.4 Debugging Your Mental Loops

1. Elizabeth Gilbert, *Eat, Pray, Love: One Woman's Search for Everything Across Italy, India and Indonesia* (New York: Penguin, 2006).

2. Michael R. Williams, *A History of Computing Technology* (New York: IEEE Computer Society Press, 1997), 248–51.

3. Thomas P. Hughes, *American Genesis: A History of the American Genius for Invention* (New York: Penguin Books, 1989), 75.

4. Simson Garfinkel, "History's Worst Software Bugs," *Wired*, Nov. 2005.

5. Sharron Ann Danis, "Rear Admiral Grace Murray Hopper," Feb. 16, 1997, http://ei.cs.vt.edu/~history/Hopper.Danis.html. Hopper also coined the phrase, "It's easier to ask forgiveness than to ask permission," the motto of any young go-getter in a risk-averse environment.

6. William Mass and Andrew Robertson, "From Textiles to Automobiles: Mechanical and Organizational Innovation in the Toyoda Enterprises, 1895–1933," *Business and Economic History* 25, No. 2 (1996): 1–35.

7. Gregory Wallace, "Toyota Has Best Value: Consumer Reports," *CNN Money*, Dec. 18, 2014: http://money.cnn.com/2014/12/18/autos/consumer-reports-best-value-toyota.

8. David Burns, *The Feeling Good Handbook* (New York: Plume, 1999), 4–7.

9. Napoleon Hill, *Think and Grow Rich* (New York: Tarcher, 2005), 249–55.

2.1 It's All in Your Mind

1. David Bodanis, "Einstein the Nobody," *NASA*, Oct. 15, 2005, http://www.pbs.org/wgbh/nova/physics/einstein-the-nobody.html.

2. A. S. Eddington, *The Nature of the Physical World* (Whitefish, MT: Kessinger Publishing, 2005), 276–81.

3. Andy Hertzfeld, "Reality Distortion Field," *Folklore*, Feb. 1981, http://www.folklore.org/StoryView.py?story=Reality_Distortion_Field.txt.

4. Vindu Goel, "Mark Zuckerberg Says Secret of His Success Is Making Lots of Mistakes," *International New York Times*, Dec. 11, 2014, http://bits.blogs.nytimes.com/2014/12/11/facebook-chief-says-secret-of-his-success-is-making-lots-of-mistakes.

5. Douglas Adams, *The Hitchhiker's Guide to the Galaxy* (London: Pan Books, 1979). I changed "chemist's" to "drugstore" for American readers.

6. Bruce Grierson, "What if Age Is Nothing but a Mind-Set?" *New York Times*, Oct. 22, 2014, http://www.nytimes.com/2014/10/26/magazine /what-if-age-is-nothing-but-a-mind-set.html.

2.2 Your Best Possible Future

1. Robert and Michele Root-Bernstein, *Sparks of Genius: The Thirteen Thinking Tools of the World's Most Creative People* (Boston: Mariner Books, 2001), 22.

2. Laura King, "The Health Benefits of Writing about Life Goals," *Personality and Social Psychology Bulletin* 27, No. 7 (July 2001): 798–807.

3. Chad Burton and Laura King, "The Health Benefits of Writing About Intensely Positive Experiences," *Journal of Research in Personality* 2, No. 38 (April 30, 2004): 150–63.

4. Brad Stone, *The Everything Store: Jeff Bezos and the Age of Amazon* (New York: Little, Brown, 2013), 76.

5. Thank you to Tim Ferriss's excellent book *The 4-Hour Workweek* (New York: Harmony, 2007) for the inspiration for these exercises.

6. Ray Dalio, *Principles* (Westport, CT: Bridgewater Associates, 2011), 14. Dalio has made this excellent book available online for free at http://www.bwater.com/Uploads/FileManager/Principles/Bridgewater -Associates-Ray-Dalio-Principles.pdf.

2.3 Creating Positive Thought Loops

1. Walter Isaacson, *Benjamin Franklin: An American Life* (New York: Simon & Schuster, 2004), 442.

2. Benjamin Franklin, *The Autobiography of Benjamin Franklin* (London: J. Parson's, 1791), 38.

3. Jonathan Schultz, "Speed Camera Lottery Wins VW Fun Theory Contest," *New York Times*, Nov. 30, 2010, http://wheels.blogs.nytimes.com /2010/11/30/speed-camera-lottery-wins-vw-fun-theory-contest.

4. Ed Nather, "The Story of Mel, A Real Programmer," Usenet, May 21, 1983, https://www.cs.utah.edu/~elb/folklore/mel.html.

5. R. A. Emmons and M. E. McCullough, "Counting Blessings Versus Burdens: An Experimental Investigation of Gratitude and Subjective Well-Being in Daily Life," *Journal of Personality and Social Psychology* 84, No. 2 (Feb. 2003), 377–38.

6. M. Scott Peck, *The Different Drum: Community Making and Peace* (New York: Touchstone, 1998), 220.

3.1 Write

1. "Thomas Edison," National Park Service, http://www.nps.gov/edis/index.htm.

2. Randall Stross, *The Wizard of Menlo Park: How Thomas Alva Edison Invented the Modern World* (New York: Crown, 2008), 154.

3. "Obesity and Overweight Fact Sheet," World Health Organization, Jan. 2015, http://www.who.int/mediacentre/factsheets/fs311/en.

4. "Adult Obesity Facts," Centers for Disease Control and Prevention, Sept. 9, 2014, http://www.cdc.gov/obesity/data/adult.html.

5. Kaiser Permanente, "Keeping a Food Diary Doubles Diet Weight Loss, Study Suggests," *ScienceDaily*, July 8, 2008, http://www.sciencedaily.com/releases/2008/07/080708080738.htm.

6. Jonah Lehrer, *Imagine: How Creativity Works* (Boston: Houghton Mifflin, 2012).

7. Richard R. Peabody was not trained as a medical doctor, but his reputation for helping so many alcoholics earned him the nickname "Dr. Peabody."

8. Richard R. Peabody, *The Common Sense of Drinking* (Boston: Little, Brown, 1935), chapter 5.

9. Michael E. Gerber, *The E-Myth Revisited: Why Most Small Businesses Don't Work and What to Do About It* (New York: HarperCollins, 2004).

10. Scott Ambler, "Just Barely Good Enough Models and Documents: An Agile Best Practice," *Agile Modeling*, http://agilemodeling.com/essays/barelyGoodEnough.html.

11. Allen B. Downey, personal interview, Nov. 7, 2014.

12. Allen B. Downey, "Free Books, Why Not?" *Green Tea Press*, http://www
     .greenteapress.com/free_books.html.

13. Allen B. Downey, "The Textbook Manifesto," *Green Tea Press*, Jan. 6,
     2010, http://www.greenteapress.com/manifesto.html.

14. Richard Wiseman, *59 Seconds: Change Your Life in Under a Minute*
     (New York: Anchor, 2010), 22.

3.2 Repeat

1. "Dilbert," *Universal Uclick*, http://www.universaluclick.com/comics
    /dilbert.

2. "Cartoonist Scott Adams," PBS, Nov. 6, 2013, http://www.pbs.org/wnet
    /tavissmiley/interviews/scott-adams.

3. Scott Adams, *The Dilbert Future: Thriving on Business Stupidity in the
    21st Century* (New York: HarperBusiness, 1998), 246–53. Also see
    Scott Adams, *How to Fail at Everything and Still Win Big: Kind of the
    Story of My Life* (New York: Portfolio, 2014), 154–57 and 224–29. Also
    see Scott Adams, "Dilbert 2.0," *Scott Adams Blog*, Oct. 13, 2008, http://
    blog.dilbert.com/post/102544366321/dilbert-2-0.

4. Ibid.

5. Ibid.

6. "Jim Carrey," IMDB, http://www.imdb.com/name/nm0000120/bio.

7. Brad Isaac, "Jerry Seinfeld's Productivity Secret," *Lifehacker*, July 24,
    2007, http://lifehacker.com/281626/jerry-seinfelds-productivity-secret.

8. F. Strack, L. L. Martin, and S. Stepper, "Inhibiting and Facilitating Con-
    ditions of the Human Smile: A Nonobtrusive Test of the Facial Feedback
    Hypothesis," *Journal of Personality and Social Psychology* 54, No. 5 (1988),
    768–77. Thanks to Richard Wiseman's *59 Seconds: Change Your Life in Un-
    der a Minute* (New York: Anchor, 2010) for this and the following study.

9. Simone Schnall and James D. Laird, "Keep Smiling: Enduring Effects
    of Facial Expressions and Postures on Emotional Experience and Mem-
    ory," *Cognition and Emotion* 17, No. 5 (2003): 787–97.

10. Dr. Joan Borysenko, *Minding the Body, Mending the Mind* (Cambridge, MA: Da Capo Press, 2007), 39.

3.3 Simulate

1. "List of Nikola Tesla Patents," *Wikipedia*, Jan. 25, 2015, http://en.wiki pedia.org/wiki/List_of_Nikola_Tesla_patents.

2. Charles Coulston Gillispie, "Tesla, Nikola," *Dictionary of Scientific Biography* (New York: Charles Scribner's Sons, 1975).

3. Nikola Tesla, "The Problem of Increasing Human Energy," *Century Illustrated*, June 1900, http://www.tfcbooks.com/tesla/1900-06-00.htm.

4. Leslie E. Gilliams, "Tesla's Plan of Electrically Treating Schoolchildren," *Popular Electricity Magazine*, 1912, http://www.teslacollection.com/tesla _articles/1912/popular_electricity_magazine/e_leslie_gilliams/tesla_s _plan_of_electrically_treating_school_children.

5. "Beam to Kill Army at 200 Miles, Tesla's Claim on 78th Birthday," *New York Times*, July 11, 1934.

6. David Hatcher Childress, *The Fantastic Inventions of Nikola Tesla* (Kempton, IL: Adventures Unlimited Press, 2014), 276.

7. Tesla, "The Problem of Increasing Human Energy."

8. "Tesla," PBS, http://www.pbs.org/tesla/ll/ll_america.html.

9. *Thomas Edison: Life of an Electrifying Man* (Biographiq, 2008), 23.

10. Anderson, 1983; Anderson & Sechler, 1986; Carroll, 1978; Gregory, Cialdini & Carpenter, 1982; Hirt & Sherman, 1985; Sherman, Skov, Hervitz & Stock, 1981; Koehler, 1991; Pham & Taylor, 1999.

11. Shelley E. Taylor, Lien B. Pham, Inna D. Rivkin, and David A. Armor, "Harnessing the Imagination: Mental Simulation, Self-Regulation, and Coping," *American Psychologist* 53, No. 4 (1998): 429–39.

12. Jack Nicklaus, *Golf My Way* (New York: Simon & Schuster, 1974), 79.

13. Alyssa Roenigk, "Lotus Pose on Two," *ESPN The Magazine*, Aug. 21, 2013, http://espn.go.com/nfl/story/_/id/9581925/seattle-seahawks-use -unusual-techniques-practice-espn-magazine.

14. Michael Gervais, PhD, http://michaelgervais.com.

15. Sir John Hargrave, "Wisdom 2.0 2014: How the Seattle Seahawks Won the Super Bowl with Mindfulness," *Wisdom 2.0*, Feb. 2013, http://wisdom2conference.tumblr.com/post/76899593413/wisdom-2-0-2014-how-the-seattle-seahawks-won-the-super.

16. Gabriele Oettingen, Caterina Bulgarella, Marlone Henderson, and Peter M. Gollwitzer, "The Self-Regulation of Goal Pursuit," in R. A. Wright, J. Greenberg, and S. S. Brehm (eds.), *Motivation and Emotion in Social Contexts: Jack Brehm's Influence on Contemporary Psychological Thought* (Mahwah, NJ: Erlbaum, 2004): 225–44.

17. Richard Wiseman, *59 Seconds*, 96.

18. T. Pyszczynski, K. Holt, and J. Greenberg, "Depression, Self-Focused Attention, and Expectancies for Positive and Negative Future Life Events for Self and Others," *Journal of Personality and Social Psychology* 52, No. 5 (May 1987): 994–1001.

19. L. Libby, E. Shaeffer, R. Eibach, and J. Slemmer, "Picture Yourself at the Polls: Visual Perspective in Mental Imagery Affects Self-Perception and Behavior," *Psychological Science* 18, No. 3 (March 18, 2007): 199–203.

3.4 Collaborate

1. Marshall Poe, "The Hive," *Atlantic Monthly*, Sept. 2006, http://www.theatlantic.com/magazine/archive/2006/09/the-hive/305118.

2. "The Early History of Nupedia and Wikipedia: A Memoir," *Slashdot*, April 18, 2005, http://features.slashdot.org/story/05/04/18/164213/%230.1_wporigins.

3. Ibid.

4. "Pixar Campus," *All About Steve Jobs*, http://allaboutstevejobs.com/pics/stevesplaces/pixar.php.

5. Jonah Lehrer, "The Steve Jobs Approach to Teamwork," *Wired*, Oct. 10, 2011, http://www.wired.com/2011/10/the-steve-jobs-approach-to-teamwork.

6. See http://www.slate.com/articles/arts/brow_beat/2014/02/february _movies_are_bad_here_s_statistical_proof_of_it.html for an aggregate Rotten Tomatoes ranking from 2000–2013, compared with average Rotten Tomatoes ranking of Pixar films taken from http://en.wikipedia .org/wiki/List_of_Pixar_films.

7. Jonah Lehrer, *Imagine: How Creativity Works*, 152.

8. Ibid., 196.

9. Steve Wozniak, *iWoz* (New York: W. W. Norton, 2006), 150.

10. Paul Freiberger and Michael Swaine, *Fire in the Valley: The Making of the Personal Computer* (New York: McGraw-Hill, 2000).

11. Jonah Lehrer, *Imagine: How Creativity Works*, 222.

12. Steven Johnson, *Where Good Ideas Come From: The Natural History of Innovation* (New York: Riverhead Trade, 2011), 58. Italics mine.

13. Gail Matthews, "Goals Research Summary," *Dominican University*, http:// www.dominican.edu/academics/ahss/undergraduate-programs-1/psych /faculty/fulltime/gailmatthews/researchsummary2.pdf.

3.5 Act

1. Charles C. Miller Memorial Apicultural Library WU, *Enquire Within upon Everything* (London: Houlston and Sons, 1903), https://archive .org/details/enquirewithinup00librgoog.

2. Sir Tim Berners-Lee, "A Brief History of the Web," *World Wide Web Consortium* (ca. 1993/1994), http://webfoundation.org/about/vision /history-of-the-web.

3. Sir Tim Berners-Lee, "Frequently Asked Questions by the Press," *W3*, http://www.w3.org/People/Berners-Lee/.

4. Sir Tim Berners-Lee, "Answers for Young People," *World Wide Web Consortium*, http://www.w3.org/People/Berners-Lee/Kids.html.

5. "Biography and Video Interview of Timothy Berners-Lee at Academy of Achievement," Achievement.org, http://www.achievement.org/autodoc /page/ber1int-1.

6. Roy Baumeister and John Tierney, *Willpower: Discovering the Greatest Human Strength* (New York: Penguin, 2012), 139–40.

7. Richard Wiseman, *59 Seconds*, 85.

8. "The Game That Can Add 10 Years to Your Life," JaneMcGonigal.com, Jan. 6, 2014, http://janemcgonigal.com/2014/01/06/transcript-the -game-that-can-add-10-years-to-your-life.